Type 2

Diabetes

Cookbook with Pictures

Easy Type 2 Diabetes Recipes and Meal Plan for Dummies

Lisa Sadler

Table of Contents

"Health is wealth" indicates the importance of being healthy but what if you're silently caught in a chronic situation that shakes you. Yes, Diabetes is a silent chronic disease. Diabetes is a situation when your pancreas makes no or insufficient insulin in the body.

There are two types of diabetes, one named Type-1 and the other is Type-2 diabetes. Type 1 diabetes is incurable but type-2 diabetes can be put in remission with a healthy lifestyle.

Type 2 diabetes mellitus is a condition in which the body controls and uses sugar (glucose) for fat. These long-term infections cause too much sugar in the arteries. Finally, high blood sugar can damage blood vessels, the nervous system, and the immune system. There is no cure for type 2 diabetes mellitus, but weight loss, eating a healthy diet, and exercising can help control the disease. If diet and exercise are not enough to control your blood sugar, you may need diabetes medication or insulin therapy.

Differences between Type-1 and Type-2 Diabetes

We know that some people develop type 1 diabetes mellitus with type 2 diabetes. And we often ask questions about the differences between them.

Type 1 diabetes and type 2 diabetes have many similarities, but there are many differences. What is the reason, who affects it and how is it managed? There are other types of diabetes, such as pregnancy and MODY.

First of all, type 1 affects 8% of all diabetics. When type 2 diabetes affects up to 90%, many people have mistaken type-2 diabetes for type 1 diabetes. It could mean that what works for one type doesn't work for another and has to explain with another reason.

The important thing to remember is that both weigh the same as each other. High blood sugar can lead to health problems, even if you have type 1 or type 2 diabetes. So, if you have both of these situations, then you need to take the necessary steps to deal with them.

The below table shows some basic knowledge about the type-1 and type-2 Diabetes.

	Type 1 Diabetes	Type 2 Diabetes
What is happening	Your Pancreas is not making insulin to dissolve glucose in cells.	The pancreas is making insulin but the amount is not sufficient for cells to work properly.
Risk Factor	No current reason is known about the type-1 occurrence.	Obesity and ethnicity put you towards the type-2 diabetes.
Symptoms	The quick appearance of symptoms	Symptoms appearance mildly and slowly
How to Manage	Taking insulin to control blood sugar	Healthy lifestyle, walking, and exercise, healthy eating, and mild medication
Prevention and cure	Not curable	Not curable but can be put into remission with a healthy lifestyle

Type 1 diabetes means you have an autoimmune disease. This means that the body attacks and destroys the cells that make insulin. It can therefore no longer produce insulin. We need insulin because it helps absorb sugar from the blood into the cells of our body. This sugar is then used for energy. Without insulin, blood sugar is too high. Type 2 diabetes is different. In type 2, the body either does not make enough insulin or does not function properly. This is called insulin resistance. According to type 1, this means the blood sugar is too high.

About Type-2 Diabetes

Type 2 diabetes mellitus, the most common type of diabetes mellitus, is a type of disease that occurs in diabetes mellitus, also called diabetes mellitus. Diabetes is your life energy and comes from the foods you eat. Insulin, a substance produced by the pancreas, helps sugar enter cells and use it for energy. In type 2 diabetes, the body either does not make enough insulin or uses insulin poorly. Too much sugar is in the blood and cannot reach the cells.

- Some of the symptoms of diabetes include;
- increased thirst and urination
- increased hunger
- feeling tired
- blurred vision
- numbness or tingling in the feet or hands
- sores that do not heal
- unexplained weight loss

Symptoms of type 2 diabetes usually appear slowly over many years and can be so minor that you may not notice it. Many people have no symptoms. Some people don't know they have the disease until they have a health problem, such as blindness or heart disease.

This cookbook and diet plan in it is here to help you manage your health well by managing your blood sugar and your health.

Formation of Type-2 Diabetes

The risk of developing type 2 diabetes is determined by some factors that can be modified and others that cannot.

1. Obesity
It is not known why some people make insulin, but obesity and lack of physical function are known to cause insulin resistance. Improving insulin resistance is important for improving type 2 diabetes. A link can also be seen in the fact that losing weight can improve the management or treatment of type 2 diabetes. In addition to obesity, the location of excess body fat is also important in determining the risk of type 2 diabetes. Levels of insulin resistance and the incidence of type 2 diabetes mellitus are highest in individuals of the "apple" type. These people carry most of their heaviest weight on their stomachs. In contrast, people with "pear" appear to have most of their weight on their hips and thighs, which is less likely to be associated with insulin resistance.

2. Gestation Period
Researchers believe gestational diabetes, type 2 diabetes that occurs during pregnancy, is caused by hormonal changes during pregnancy, including genetics and lifestyle. Hormones produced by the NIH placental network externally activate insulin resistance, which occurs in all women after pregnancy. Most women can produce enough insulin during pregnancy to beat insulin resistance, but some do not. Gestational diabetes mellitus occurs when the pancreas does not produce enough insulin. As with type 2 diabetes mellitus, obesity is also associated with gestational diabetes. Overweight women can avoid insulin during pregnancy. Excessive weight gain during pregnancy can also cause diabetes. Hormonal changes, weight gain, and family

history all contribute towards gestational diabetes but sometimes it is just temporary and ended after delivery.

3. Hypertension

High blood pressure, or hypertension, can also cause type 2 diabetes. Hypertension can cause or worsen many types of diabetes, including diabetes mellitus and kidney infections. Most people with diabetes eventually develop high blood pressure as well as other heart and circulatory problems. Diabetes damages the arteries and makes them targeted for a hardening called arteriosclerosis. This can lead to high blood pressure which, if left untreated, can lead to problems such as blood vessel damage, heart attack, and kidney failure.

The combination of high blood pressure and type 2 diabetes is particularly deadly and can increase the risk of heart disease or stroke. Diabetic retinopathy can lead to blindness. Some people can improve their type 2 diabetes and high blood pressure with lifestyle changes, but most need medication. Depending on their general health, some people may need more than one medicine to control their blood pressure.

4. Other Causes

Genetic mutations, NIH external link, other, damage to the pancreas, and certain medicines may also cause diabetes.

Genes And Family History

Family history puts women at risk for gestational diabetes. This indicates that the seeds are playing a role. Genetic studies explain why this problem is more prevalent among African Americans, American Indians, Asians, and Hispanics. Diabetes alone is caused by a mutation or a change in a gene. These mutations are usually passed down through the family, but sometimes genetic mutations do occur. Most of these mutations cause insulin levels to drop, leading to diabetes. Type 1 diabetes is more common in children and mature-onset diabetes mellitus (MODY). Neonatal diabetes develops at 6 months. NIH cystic fibrosis externally causes thick mucus in the scar tissue which can prevent the pancreas from making enough insulin. Hemochromatosis issue causes too much iron in the body. If left untreated, iron can build up and cause cuts and other infections.

Hormonal Diseases

Diabetes is caused by a hormonal imbalance. The pancreas produces the hormone insulin, which is absorbed into the blood by fat, muscle, and liver cells and used for energy. Insulin also helps other metabolic processes in the body.

If you have type 2 diabetes, your body will fight off insulin. In response, the cutter works harder to produce more insulin to lower blood sugar, but it doesn't store it. The result is uncontrolled diabetes.

For example;

Hormonal changes during menopause affect blood sugar levels, and postmenopausal women may experience faster changes in blood sugar levels if they have diabetes. The weight gain associated with pregnancy may require changes in blood sugar levels, and low hormones can interfere with sleep, making it more difficult to control blood sugar. Women with diabetes are also more likely to have sex than usual. The reason is that the disease is associated with damage to the cells of the vagina.

Men experience similar issues when their bodies produce low testosterone, including muscle loss and decreased sex drive. However, many people are unaware that low testosterone can also lead to insulin resistance.

Some other hormonal problems cause the body to make too many hormones, sometimes leading to insulin resistance and diabetes.

Cushing's syndrome occurs when the body makes too much cortisol, often referred to as a "stress hormone". Acromegaly occurs when the body makes too many hormones. Hyperthyroidism occurs when the thyroid gland overproduces thyroid hormone.

Damage to or Removal of the Pancreas

Pancreatitis, leukemia, and injury can damage any beta cells or reduce their ability to produce insulin, leading to diabetes. When pancreatic cancer is eliminated, beta cells disappear, leading to diabetes.

How to Prevent and Control Diabetes

If you are at risk for diabetes, you can prevent or delay diabetes. Most of all you need to do are stay healthy. Therefore, this change has other health benefits as well. You can lower your risk of getting other illnesses and make you feel better and stronger. Here are the changes:

Develop Good Habits

Type-2 diabetes can be put to remission by developing good habits like a healthy lifestyle, healthy eating, and proper medication. You should have quit smoking and drinking which lead you towards managing active metabolic activities that can help you to reduce your diabetes and allow you to live a healthy lifestyle with this chronic disease.

Some of the following activities help you to manage type-2 diabetes. Following are;

Cut of Refined Carbs and Sugar from the Diet

Avoiding these foods can help lower your risk, as eating a diet high in good carbohydrates and sugar can increase blood sugar and insulin levels, which can lead to hypoglycemia. Your body very quickly breaks down sugars and carbohydrate-rich foods into small pieces that your brain absorbs. The result is high blood sugar. Replacing sugary foods or foods low in carbohydrates can help control diabetes. People who eat a lot of carbohydrates quickly are more likely to have type 2 diabetes than those who take less.

Drink a Lot of Water

Water is the best drink for you. Helps reduce the risk of diabetes, which can increase blood sugar. Studies show that drinking helps the body make the best insulin and control blood sugar. Water reduces cravings for sweet and salty drinks which can help control blood sugar.

Quit Smoking

Smoking is associated with an increased risk of diabetes, especially in heavy smokers. Smoking has been shown to cause or worsen serious illnesses, including heart disease, emphysema, lung cancer, breast cancer, prostate cancer, and indigestion. You may have a risk for type 2 diabetes. Quitting smoking has been shown to reduce these risks over time.

Take Coffee and Tea

While water should be your first drink, research shows that including coffee or tea in your diet can help prevent diabetes. Studies indicate that daily coffee intake reduces the risk of type 2 diabetes. Coffee and tea contain antioxidants called polyphenols, which can help prevent diabetes. Green tea also contains a special antioxidant called epigallocatechin gallate (EGCG), which has been shown to reduce the release of blood sugar from the liver and increase insulin secretion.

Minimized Processed Food Intake

Cutting back on your diet and focusing on healthy whole foods can help lower your risk for diabetes. One easy step that you can take to improve your health is to cut back on your processed foods. It caused all kinds of health problems, including heart disease, obesity, and diabetes. Cutting back on fatty foods, whole grains, and supplements can help lower your risk for diabetes. It is part of fruits, vegetables, berries, and other food crops.

Eat High Fiber Diet

Eating good fiber with every meal can help lower your risk of diabetes by preventing high blood sugar and insulin levels. Eating fiber helps with stomach health and weight management. Fiber can be divided into two groups: soluble and insoluble. Soluble fiber can absorb water, while insoluble fiber does not.

Intake of Vitamin D

Eating a diet rich in vitamin D or taking supplements can help lower your risk of diabetes by improving your vitamin D levels. Vitamin D is important for managing diabetes. Studies have shown that not getting enough vitamin D or having low blood pressure increases the risk of developing all types of diabetes. When people become malnourished by taking vitamin D, it improves the function of insulin-producing cells, normalizes blood sugar levels, and reduces the risk of diabetes. Oily fish and cod liver oil are good sources of vitamin D. Sun exposure can increase the amount of vitamin D in the blood. However, for many people, it is necessary to supplement 2,000 to 4,000 IU of vitamin D per day to achieve and maintain high levels.

Regular Exercises

Daily physical activities, such as exercising and walking, help your brain break down the sugars and fats in your body by digesting food and releasing insulin from your pancreas. Exercise increases insulin sensitivity in the brain. So when you exercise, you need less insulin to control your blood sugar. Aerobic exercise, high-intensity exercise, and strength training can help obese people lower blood sugar and control type 2 diabetes. Regular physical activity increases insulin secretion and sensitivity, which helps prevent type 2 diabetes and lower blood sugar.

Dietary Requirements for Type-2 Diabetes

People with type-2 diabetes find it difficult to get enough sugar to the brain. When the sugar does not reach the desired level, the sugar in the blood rises. which can lead to problems such as kidneys, brain, eye damage, and heart disease.

The best diet for type 2 diabetes includes simple carbohydrates such as brown rice, whole grains, quinoa, oatmeal, fruits, vegetables, beans, and lentils. Foods to avoid include simple carbohydrates such as sugar, pasta, white bread, flour, cookies, and pastries.

Foods that do not have a glycemic load (index) raise blood sugar levels only slightly and are a better choice for diabetics. Effective blood sugar control can help prevent the long-term problems of type 2 diabetes. Fat does not have a direct effect on blood sugar, but it can help slow the absorption of carbohydrates.

Protein provides constant energy with little cause on blood sugar. It can help to even blood sugar levels and ease sugar cravings. Foods high in protein include beans, legumes, eggs, seafood, dairy products, soybeans, soybeans, lean meats, and chicken. Diabetic "superfoods" contain chia seeds, wild salmon, cinnamon white balsamic vinegar, and lentils. They help you to maintain diabetes and fulfill you as well.

A healthy diet includes lots of vegetables, a limited amount of sugar, and red meat. Dietary recommendations for people with type 2 diabetes include a vegetarian or vegan diet with the importance of exercise. The diet of people with type 2 diabetes includes a diet that is low in glycemic load, high in vegetables, and high in vegetable fats and proteins.

In type-2 diabetes, Which foods are not allowed to eat: soft drinks (regularly and on a diet), refined sugars, processed carbohydrates, saturated fat, fatty junk food, foods high in fat, fruit juices high in fructose, sweets, and all processed foods.

What to Eat

You can follow a variety of diets and diets to meet your health needs. For type 2 diabetes, you need to choose foods that contain nutritious foods that can help provide your body with the fiber, vitamins, and minerals it needs. You should eat a diversity of heart oils, including monounsaturated and polyunsaturated fatty acids. These fatty acids can help you to maintain a healthy heart by lowering cholesterol.

Likewise, eating a diet high in fiber can improve blood sugar control and allow you to eat longer, preventing you from overating when you're not hungry. The diet should be safe and easy to follow as well as tasty at the same time. A diet that is restricted or does not suit your lifestyle can be difficult to manage in the long term.

Here are some examples of foods you should include in your diet.

- **Fruits:** apples, oranges, strawberries, melons, pears, and peaches.
- **Vegetables:** cauliflower, cabbage, cucumber, pumpkin, etc.
- **Whole grains:** quinoa, couscous, oats, brown rice, Faro
- **Beans:** beans, lentils, and chickpeas
- **Nuts:** almonds, walnuts, pistachios, macadamia nuts, cashews
- **Seeds:** chia seeds, pumpkin seeds, flax seeds, hemp seeds
- **Foods rich in** Protein: lean chicken, seafood, lean meats, beans, tempeh
- **Heart-healthy fats:** olive oil, avocado, canola oil, sesame oil
- **Drinks:** water, black coffee, unsweetened tea, soup

What to Avoid

There aren't many foods that you should avoid completely when you have type 2 diabetes. However, some foods have more choices than others in terms of healthy nutrients. This means that it is rich in vitamins and minerals and low in fat.

Limiting your intake of foods high in fat, and sugar can help improve blood sugar control and prevent the health effects associated with diabetes.

Here are some of the foods you should limit or avoid in your diet with type-2 diabetes:

• **Fatty meats:** beef, lamb, chicken, black chicken
• **Fatty foods:** whole milk, butter, cheese, sour cream
• **Sweets:** candies, cookies, toast, ice cream, candies
• **Non-alcoholic drinks:** non-alcoholic drinks, tea sweeteners, processed juices
• **Sweeteners:** sugar, brown sugar, honey, maple syrup, molasses
• **Processed foods:** chips, microwave popcorn, processed meats, ready meals
• **Fatty foods:** short vegetables, fried foods, dairy-free coffee, semi-hydrogenated fats

Coconut Porridge

Prep Time: 10 Minutes
Cook Time: 10 Minutes
Serves: 4

Ingredients:
- 4 cups unsweetened vanilla almond milk
- 1 cup unsweetened coconut, grated
- 8 teaspoons coconut flour

Preparation:
1. Put the grated coconut in a saucepan over medium-high heat until lightly toasted. Make sure it doesn't burn.
2. Add the milk and bring it to a boil.
3. Slowly add the flour, stirring constantly, and simmer and stir until the mixture thickens (about 5 minutes).
4. Remove the pan from the heat; the mixture will thicken as it cools. Pour the porridge into bowls.
5. Serve and enjoy.

Serving Suggestion: Top with berries of your choice.

Variation Tip: Substitute almond milk with any other nut milk of your choice.

Nutritional Information per Serving:
Calories 231 | Fat 14g | Sodium 184mg | Carbs 21g | Fiber 13g | Sugar 4g | Protein 6g

Pomegranate Porridge

Prep Time: 10 Minutes
Cook Time: 8 Minutes
Serves: 2

Ingredients:
- ¼ cup oatmeal
- 1 cup pomegranate seeds
- 1 cup pomegranate juice

Preparation:
1. Mix the oatmeal and pomegranate juice in a saucepan over medium heat.
2. Allow the mixture to simmer for 5 minutes.
3. Remove the pan from the heat, add the pomegranate seeds, and stir the porridge well.
4. Serve and enjoy.

Serving Suggestion: Top with maple syrup.

Variation Tip: Substitute pomegranate with passion fruit.

Nutritional Information per Serving:
Calories 155| Fat 1.2g | Sodium 17mg | Carbs 37.4g | Fiber 2.5g | Sugar 15.6g | Protein 1.9g

Cauliflower Oatmeal

Prep Time: 10 minutes
Cook Time: 10 minutes
Servings: 4

Ingredients:
- 1 tablespoon peanut butter
- ½ teaspoon stevia
- 2 cups cauliflower rice
- 1 teaspoon cinnamon
- 2 strawberries, sliced
- 1 cup unsweetened almond milk

Preparation:
1. Put the cauliflower rice in a pot along with the milk, cinnamon, and stevia and let it reach a boil.
2. Stir occasionally until the mixture thickens.
3. Remove the pot from the heat and dish out the cauliflower oatmeal into bowls.
4. Drizzle with creamy peanut butter before serving.

Serving Suggestions: Serve topped with strawberries, blueberries, and coconut flakes.

Variation Tip: You can also use soy milk.

Nutritional Information per Serving:
Calories: 254|Fat: 11.2g|Sat Fat: 0.5g|Carbohydrates: 29.1g|Fiber: 5.1g|Sugar: 0.7g|Protein: 5.5g

Bulgur Porridge

Prep Time: 10 Minutes
Cook Time: 15 Minutes
Serves: 4
Ingredients:
• 4 cups almond milk
• 1 cup bulgur
• ⅓ cup dried cherries
• ¼ tablespoon salt
• 1 banana, sliced
• ⅓ cup dried apricots, coarsely chopped
• ½ cup almonds, sliced
Preparation:
1. Put the milk, bulgur, dried cherries, and salt in a large saucepan. Bring to a boil.
2. Reduce the heat to low and simmer for about 10–15 minutes, constantly stirring, until the oatmeal is tender.
3. Divide among 4 bowls and serve.
Serving Suggestion: Garnish with the chopped apricots, banana slices, and sliced almonds.
Variation Tip: Substitute almonds with pistachios.
Nutritional Information per Serving:
Calories 340 | Fat 6.7g | Sodium 404mg | Carbs 21g | Fiber 5g | Sugar 2g | Protein 15g

Buckwheat Crepes

Prep Time: 10 Minutes
Cook Time: 15 Minutes
Serves: 8
Ingredients:
• 1 cup buckwheat flour
• ⅓ cup whole grain flour
• 1 egg, beaten
• 1 cup skim milk
• 1 teaspoon olive oil

• ½ teaspoon ground cinnamon
Preparation:
1. Mix all the ingredients in a mixing bowl using a whisk until you get a smooth batter.
2. Heat a non-stick skillet on high heat for 3 minutes.
3. Using a ladle, pour a small amount of batter into the skillet and flatten it into the shape of a crepe.
4. Cook the batter for 1 minute, then flip it over. Cook it for 30 seconds more.
5. Repeat the same steps with the remaining batter.
Serving Suggestion: Top with fresh berries.
Variation Tip: Substitute buckwheat flour with oat flour.
Nutritional Information per Serving:
Calories 122 | Fat 2.2g | Sodium 34mg | Carbs 141.g | Fiber 2.2g | Sugar 2g | Protein 5.7g

Chickpea Flour Omelet

Prep Time: 10 Minutes
Cook Time: 20 Minutes
Serves: 1
Ingredients:
• 1 cup chickpea flour
• ⅓ cup nutritional yeast
• 3 green onions, finely chopped
• 4 ounces mushrooms, sautéed
• ½ teaspoon onion powder
• ¼ teaspoon black pepper
• ½ teaspoon garlic powder
• ½ teaspoon baking soda
• ¼ teaspoon white pepper
Preparation:
1. Combine the onion powder, white pepper, chickpea flour, garlic powder, black and white pepper, baking soda, and yeast in a bowl.
2. Add 1 cup of water and mix well until a smooth batter forms.
3. Heat a non-stick skillet over medium heat and add the batter like you would a pancake.
4. Sprinkle some green onion and mushrooms on top of the batter and cook for about 5 minutes.
5. Flip the omelet over and cook for another 3–5 minutes.
6. Slide the cooked omelet onto a serving plate and sprinkle with the remaining green onion and mushrooms.
Serving Suggestion: Serve the omelet with hot sauce and salsa.
Variation Tip: Substitute chickpea flour with almond flour.
Nutritional Information per Serving:
Calories 150 | Fat 1.9g | Sodium 230mg | Carbs 2.4g | Fiber 2.2g | Sugar 0g | Protein 10.2g

Peach Pancakes

Prep Time: 10 Minutes
Cook Time: 10 Minutes
Serves: 6
Ingredients:
• 1 cup whole-wheat flour
• 1 egg, beaten
• 1 teaspoon vanilla extract
• 2 peaches, chopped
• 1 tablespoon olive oil
• ½ teaspoon baking powder
• 1 teaspoon apple cider vinegar
• ¼ cup skim milk
Preparation:
1. Mix the eggs, whole-wheat flour, vanilla extract, baking powder, apple cider vinegar, and skim milk in a mixing bowl.
2. Heat the olive oil over medium heat in a non-stick skillet.
3. Pour some of the prepared batter into the skillet and flatten it into the shape of a pancake.
4. Cook the pancake for 2 minutes on each side over medium-low heat.
5. Repeat for the remaining batter.
6. Serve and enjoy!
Serving Suggestion: Top the cooked pancakes with the chopped peaches.
Variation Tip: Substitute peaches with apricots.
Nutritional Information per Serving:
Calories 129 | Fat 3g | Sodium 39mg | Carbs 21.5g | Fiber1.3g | Sugar 5.4g | Protein 3.9g

Blueberry Overnight Oats

Prep Time: 5 Minutes + Overnight
Cook Time: 0 Minutes
Serves: 2
Ingredients:
• ½ cup nut milk of your choice
• ½ cup plain Greek yogurt
• ½ cup gluten-free rolled oats
• 2 tablespoons chia seeds
• Juice and zest of 1 lemon
• 1 tablespoon maple syrup
• 1 teaspoon pure vanilla extract
• Pinch of sea salt
• 1 cup blueberries
Preparation:
1. Combine the ingredients except for the blueberries in a medium-size bowl.
2. Fold in the blueberries, cover, and refrigerate overnight.
Serving Suggestion: Garnish with mint leaves.
Variation Tip: Double the recipe, evenly divide the ingredients among four jars, seal, and refrigerate for a convenient grab-and-go breakfast.
Nutritional Information per Serving:
Calories 283 | Fat 6g | Sodium 133mg | Carbs 42g | Fiber 10g | Sugar 17g | Protein 10g

Egg Muffins with Turkey and Bacon

Prep Time: 15 minutes
Cook Time: 28 minutes
Servings: 6
Ingredients:
• 6 ounces yellow onion, finely chopped
• 4 ounces baby spinach
• 2 garlic cloves, finely chopped
• 24 slices lean turkey bacon
• 6 eggs
• 5 ounces red bell pepper, chopped
• 1 jalapeño chili, finely chopped
• 40 ounces egg whites
• 5 ounces lean turkey sausage, chopped
• Salt and black pepper, to taste
Preparation:
1. Preheat the oven to 350°F and lightly grease a muffin pan.
2. Place a bacon slice inside each muffin mold and add a little spinach to each.
3. Sauté the onions in some oil in a hot skillet for 3 minutes until they're translucent.
4. Divide the cooked onions evenly between the muffin molds, placing them over the spinach.
5. Add the sausage and bell pepper on top.
6. Combine the egg whites, whole eggs, salt, and black pepper in a bowl and whisk well.
7. Drizzle the egg mixture into the muffin molds and place them on the middle rack of the preheated oven.
8. Bake for 25 minutes.
9. Dish out and serve.
Serving Suggestions: Serve along with hot tea.
Variation Tip: You can use fresh berries too.
Nutritional Information per Serving:
Calories: 313|Fat: 7.2g|Sat Fat: 1.4g|Carbohydrates: 16.4g|Fiber: 3.6g|Sugar: 8.1g|Protein: 41.8g

Asparagus Omelet

Prep Time: 10 Minutes
Cook Time: 10 Minutes
Serves: 2

Ingredients:
- 3 ounces asparagus, boiled and chopped
- ¼ teaspoon ground paprika
- ½ teaspoon ground cumin
- 3 eggs, beaten
- 2 tablespoons skim milk
- 1 teaspoon avocado oil

Preparation:
1. Heat the avocado oil in a non-stick skillet over medium heat.
2. Meanwhile, combine the ground paprika and ground cumin in a bowl.
3. Add the eggs and milk and mix until well combined.
4. Pour the mixture into the hot skillet and cook it for 2 minutes.
5. Add the chopped asparagus and cover the skillet with a lid.
6. Cook the omelet for 5 minutes on low heat.
7. Serve immediately and enjoy.

Serving Suggestion: Serve with sliced tomatoes.
Variation Tip: Substitute avocado oil with olive oil.
Nutritional Information per Serving:
Calories 115 | Fat 7.2g | Sodium 101mg | Carbs 3.4g | Fiber 1.2g | Sugar 2.1g | Protein 9.9g

Strawberry and Ricotta Pancakes

Prep Time: 10 Minutes
Cook Time: 20 Minutes
Serves: 4

Ingredients:
- 1¼ cups nut milk of your choice
- ½ cup ricotta cheese
- 1 large egg
- 1 tablespoon canola oil
- 1 tablespoon freshly squeezed lemon juice
- ½ teaspoon pure vanilla extract
- 1¼ cups whole-wheat flour

- 1 tablespoon sugar
- 2 teaspoons baking powder
- ¼ teaspoon salt
- Canola oil, for cooking
- 1 cup strawberries, sliced

Preparation:
1. Whisk the milk, ricotta, egg, oil, lemon juice, and vanilla in a large bowl until well blended.
2. Whisk in the flour, sugar, baking powder, and salt until combined.
3. Heat a griddle or large skillet on medium heat and lightly grease it with oil.
4. Reduce the heat to medium-low and, working in batches, add the batter in ¼-cup measures.
5. Cook until the edges of the pancakes are firm and golden, about 2 minutes
6. Scatter the strawberries on top of each, and flip.
7. Cook the pancakes for 1 minute more until cooked through, transfer them to a plate, and cover loosely with aluminum foil to keep them warm.
8. Repeat with the remaining batter and serve.

Serving Suggestion: Serve with strawberry sauce.
Variation Tip: Instead of cooking the strawberries into the pancakes, you can use the fruit as a topping instead.
Nutritional Information per Serving:
Calories 285 | Fat 9g | Sodium 220mg | Carbs 40g | Fiber 5g | Sugar 9g | Protein 12g

Cottage Cheese Pancakes

Prep Time: 10 minutes
Cook Time: 10 minutes
Servings: 4

Ingredients:
- 2 teaspoons vanilla extract
- 4 egg whites
- 3 teaspoons raw stevia
- ½ cup oats
- 2 cup low-fat cottage cheese

Preparation:
1. Mix the cottage cheese with the egg whites using a blender.
2. Add the oats, vanilla extract, and stevia and blend until well incorporated.
3. Grease a skillet with cooking spray and fry the batter (in batches) on medium heat, flipping the pancakes halfway through the cooking time.
4. Serve warm.

Serving Suggestions: Serve sprinkled with cinnamon.
Variation Tip: You can use any sweetener you prefer.
Nutritional Information per Serving:
Calories: 164|Fat: 2.9g|Sat Fat: 1.5g|Carbohydrates: 11.5g|Fiber: 1g|Sugar: 1g|Protein: 20.5g

Egg Muffins

Prep Time: 5 minutes
Cook Time: 12 minutes
Servings: 4

Ingredients:
• 1 cup cheddar cheese, shredded
• ¼ cup bacon, cooked and crumbled
• 1½ tablespoons almond milk, unsweetened
• 2 cherry tomatoes, chopped
• ½ cup mixed greens, chopped
• ¼ teaspoon garlic salt
• ⅛ cup red onion, chopped
• 4 egg yolks

Preparation:
1. Preheat the oven to 400°F and lightly grease a muffin pan.
2. Mix the egg yolks, mixed greens, tomatoes, and onions in a bowl.
3. Add the bacon, cheese, almond milk, and garlic salt and mix well.
4. Pour the egg mixture evenly into the muffin molds.
5. Bake for about 12 minutes in the preheated oven.
6. Sprinkle with cheddar cheese and keep aside for 2 minutes before serving.

Serving Suggestions: Serve alongside your favorite smoothie.
Variation Tip: You can also use unsweetened coconut milk.
Nutritional Information per Serving:
Calories: 206|Fat: 14.8g|Sat Fat: 7.8g|Carbohydrates: 7g|Fiber: 1.9g|Sugar: 2.8g|Protein: 13g

Whipped Cottage Cheese Breakfast Bowl

Prep Time: 5 minutes
Cook Time: 0 minutes
Servings: 6

Ingredients:
• ¼ ounces unsweetened coconut flakes
• 2 tablespoons blackberries
• ½ ounces hazelnuts
• 2 tablespoons pomegranate seeds
• ¼ cup low-fat cottage cheese

Preparation:
1. Mix the cottage cheese, pomegranate seeds, coconut flakes, and blackberries using a blender until creamy.
2. Top the smoothie with the hazelnuts, then refrigerate to serve it chilled.

Serving Suggestions: Serve topped with blackberries, coconut flakes, and pomegranate seeds.
Variation Tip: You can also use blueberries as a substitute for blackberries.
Nutritional Information per Serving:
Calories: 63|Fat: 2.1g|Sat Fat: 0.6g|Carbohydrates: 10g|Fiber: 0.9g|Sugar: 7.3g|Protein: 2.1g

Smoked Salmon and Cream Cheese Wraps

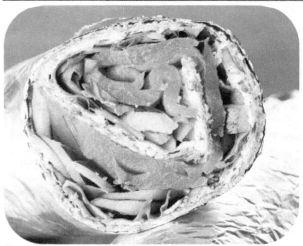

Prep Time: 15 minutes
Cook Time: 0 minutes
Servings: 2

Ingredients:
• ½ teaspoon arugula
• 2½ ounces red onion, finely sliced
• 1 teaspoon fresh basil
• 4 ounces smoked salmon
• Salt and black pepper, to taste
• 2 low-carb flour tortillas
• 4 teaspoons low-fat cream cheese

Preparation:
1. Combine the cream cheese, basil, and pepper in a bowl. Mix well.
2. Warm the tortillas in a preheated oven or microwave and spread the cream cheese mixture on top.
3. Top with the salmon, arugula, and onion.
4. Roll the tortillas and serve!

Serving Suggestions: Serve with your choice of dip.
Variation Tip: You can also use fresh cilantro.
Nutritional Information per Serving:
Calories: 235|Fat: 5.7g|Sat Fat: 1.6g|Carbohydrates: 26.5g|Fiber: 8.2g|Sugar: 6.4g|Protein: 19.4g

Quinoa Breakfast Bowl

Prep Time: 5 minutes
Cook Time: 15 minutes
Servings: 4
Ingredients:
• 2 cups low-fat coconut milk
• 1 cup quinoa, rinsed
Preparation:
1. Add the milk to a large saucepan over medium heat and let it reach a boil, occasionally stirring.
2. Add the quinoa and reduce the heat to low.
3. Secure the lid and simmer for about 15 minutes.
4. Remove the pan from the heat and fluff the quinoa with a fork before serving.
Serving Suggestions: Serve topped with peaches and raspberries.
Variation Tip: You can also use unsweetened almond milk.
Nutritional Information per Serving:
Calories: 217|Fat: 5g|Sat Fat: 2g|Carbohydrates: 33g|Fiber: 3g|Sugar: 6g|Protein: 10g

French Toast with Fruit

Prep Time: 10 Minutes
Cook Time: 20 Minutes
Serves: 8
Ingredients:
• 4 eggs
• 4 tablespoons skim milk
• 1½ cups blueberries
• ½ cup orange juice
• 1 teaspoon orange zest
• 16 slices whole-wheat bread,
• 3 tablespoons Splenda, divided
• ⅛ teaspoon salt
• Non-stick cooking spray
• 1 banana, sliced
• 1½ cups strawberries, sliced
Preparation:

1. Preheat the oven to 400℉.
2. Coat a large baking sheet with the cooking spray.
3. Combine the blueberries and two tablespoons of Splenda in a small bowl.
4. Arrange 8 slices of bread on a clean work surface. Evenly divide the berry mixture onto them.
5. Place the remaining slices on top of each, then slightly flatten.
6. Combine the skim milk, salt, and eggs in a small mixing dish.
7. Carefully dip the bread slices into this egg mixture and place them on the prepared baking sheet.
8. Cook for 7–12 minutes per side in the oven, or until gently browned.
9. Meanwhile, heat the orange juice, orange zest, and 1 tablespoon of Splenda in a small saucepan over medium heat.
10. Serve.
Serving Suggestion: Top the French toast with the orange sauce, banana, and strawberry slices
Variation Tip: Feel free to add other fruits.
Nutritional Information per Serving:
Calories 208 | Fat 10g | Sodium 315mg | Carbs 20g | Fiber 2g | Sugar 14g | Protein 7g

Chocolate Chia Seed Pudding with Almond Milk

Prep Time: 1 hour
Cook Time: 0 minutes
Servings: 3
Ingredients:
• ½ cup stevia
• 3 cups unsweetened almond milk
• 1 cup cocoa powder
• 1 cup chia seeds
• Salt, to taste
Preparation:
1. Mix the cocoa powder with all the other ingredients in a bowl.
2. Whisk until smooth, then cover the bowl.
3. Keep the bowl in the refrigerator for an hour.
4. Serve chilled and enjoy!
Serving Suggestions: Serve topped with strawberries.
Variation Tip: You can also use soy milk.
Nutritional Information per Serving:
Calories: 150|Fat: 10.2g|Sat Fat: 2.8g|Carbohydrates: 21.7g|Fiber: 12.8g|Sugar: 0.5g|Protein: 7.8g

Baked Carrot

Prep Time: 10 Minutes
Cook Time: 20 Minutes
Serves: 1
Ingredients:
• 3 ounces carrots, peeled and cut into thin slices diagonally
• ½ tablespoon extra-virgin olive oil
• ¼ teaspoon arrowroot starch
• ⅛ teaspoons red chili powder
• ⅛ teaspoon ground cinnamon
• Salt and black pepper, to taste
Preparation:
1. Preheat the oven to 425℉. Using parchment paper, line a rimmed baking sheet.
2. Combine all of the ingredients in a mixing bowl.
3. Arrange the coated carrot sticks in a single layer on the prepared baking sheet and bake for 20 minutes, tossing halfway through.
4. When done, serve and enjoy.
Serving Suggestion: Top with chopped cilantro.
Variation Tip: Omit the red chili powder for a milder taste.
Nutritional Information per Serving:
Calories 99 | Fat 7.1g | Sodium 85mg | Carbs 8g | Fiber 2.4g | Sugar 4g | Protein 0.8g

Baked Banana Chips

Prep Time: 10 Minutes
Cook Time: 2 Hours
Serves: 2
Ingredients:
• 1 teaspoon lemon juice
• 2 just-ripe bananas, sliced

Preparation:
1. Preheat the oven to 225℉.
2. Line a baking sheet with parchment paper.
3. Arrange the banana slices evenly over the baking sheet in a single layer.
4. Brush the lemon juice over the slices.
5. Bake the chips for 90 minutes in the preheated oven.
6. Allow the bananas chips to cool for at least 5 minutes before eating.
Serving Suggestion: Serve with a tamarind dip.
Variation Tip: Add chili powder for a varied taste.
Nutritional Information per Serving:
Calories 264 | Fat 0.4g | Sodium 2mg | Carbs 27.2g | Fiber 12g | Sugar 11g | Protein 1.3g

Paprika Chickpeas

Prep Time: 10 Minutes
Cook Time: 45 Minutes
Serves: 1
Ingredients:
• 2 tablespoons cooked chickpeas
• 1 garlic clove, minced
• ⅛ teaspoon dried oregano, crushed
• Pinch of ground cumin
• Pinch of smoked paprika
• Pinch of cayenne pepper
• Salt, as required
• ½ teaspoon olive oil
Preparation:
1. Preheat the oven to 400℉. Spray a baking sheet with cooking oil.
2. Arrange the cooked chickpeas in a single layer on the prepared baking sheet and roast them in the preheated oven for about 30 minutes, tossing them every 10 minutes.
3. Meanwhile, combine the garlic, oregano, and spices in a small mixing bowl.
4. When the cooking time is up, remove the baking sheet from the oven.
5. Drizzle the oil over the chickpeas and sprinkle with the garlic mixture.
6. Toss well and cook for another 10–15 minutes.
7. Turn off the oven but leave the baking sheet in for another 10 minutes.
8. Remove the chickpeas from the oven and set them aside to cool completely before serving.
Serving Suggestion: Serve with a drizzle of lemon juice.
Variation Tip: Omit cayenne pepper for a milder snack.
Nutritional Information per Serving:
Calories 59 | Fat 2.8g | Sodium 158mg | Carbs 7.3g | Fiber1.6g | Sugar 0.1g | Protein 1.6g

Spinach Chips

Prep Time: 10 Minutes
Cook Time: 8 Minutes
Serves: 1
Ingredients:
• 1 cup fresh spinach leaves
• ½ teaspoon extra-virgin olive oil
• Salt, to taste
Preparation:
1. Preheat the oven to 325℉. Line a baking sheet with parchment paper.
2. Add the spinach leaves to a bowl and sprinkle with the olive oil; use your hands to rub the spinach leaves until they're well coated.
3. Arrange the leaves in a single layer on the prepared baking sheet and bake in the preheated oven for 8 minutes.
4. When done, remove the spinach chips from the oven and set them aside to cool before serving.
Serving Suggestion: Serve with your favorite dip.
Variation Tip: Feel free to add more seasoning to your chips.
Nutritional Information per Serving:
Calories 27 | Fat 2.5g | Sodium 179mg | Carbs 1.1g | Fiber 0.7g | Sugar 0.1g | Protein 0.9g

Parsnip Fries

Prep Time: 10 Minutes
Cook Time: 10 Minutes
Serves: 1
Ingredients:
• 2 ounces parsnip, peeled and sliced
• 1 teaspoon olive oil
• Salt, to taste
Preparation:
1. Preheat the oven to 390℉. Line a baking sheet with parchment paper.

2. Toss the parsnip slices in the oil in a mixing bowl, ensuring they're well-coated.
3. Arrange the parsnip slices in a single layer on the prepared baking sheet and bake in the preheated oven for 30 minutes, turning the slices halfway through.
4. Serve immediately.
Serving Suggestion: Serve with tomato sauce.
Variation Tip: Substitute parsnip with sweet potato.
Nutritional Information per Serving:
Calories 83 | Fat 4.8g | Sodium 161mg | Carbs 10.2g | Fiber 2.8g | Sugar 2.7g | Protein 0.7g

Baked Potatoes with Veggies and Nuts

Prep Time: 5 minutes
Cook Time: 25 minutes
Servings: 2
Ingredients:
• ½ cup reduced-sodium vegetable stock
• ½ carrot, finely chopped
• 2 tablespoons soy milk
• 2 potatoes
• ½ celery, diced
• ⅛ cup cashew nuts, toasted
• ⅛ cup red lentils
Preparation:
1. Preheat the oven to 400°F. Wrap each potato in foil, place them on a baking sheet, and cook in the preheated oven for an hour.
2. Meanwhile, put the lentils, carrot, celery, and stock in a saucepan and let the mixture reach a boil over medium-high heat.
3. Reduce the heat, cover the pan, and cook for another 10 minutes.
4. Remove the baked potatoes from the oven and remove the foil. Scoop out the flesh, leaving a hole for the filling.
5. Combine the potato flesh with the lentil mixture and soy milk in a bowl.
6. Add the filling to each potato and cover them in foil.
7. Place back in the oven and bake for about 15 minutes.
8. Serve hot and enjoy!
Serving Suggestions: Serve topped with cashews and fresh parsley.
Variation Tip: You can also use macadamia nuts.
Nutritional Information per Serving:
Calories: 264|Fat: 4.6g|Sat Fat: 0.9g|Carbohydrates: 46.1g|Fiber: 9.8g|Sugar: 4.7g|Protein: 8.7g

Jicama Snack

Prep Time: 10 Minutes
Cook Time: 0 Minutes
Serves: 4

Ingredients:
- 2 tablespoons chili powder
- 2 tablespoons lime juice
- 1 cucumber, sliced
- 1 medium jicama, cut and peeled

Preparation:
1. Place the jicama and sliced cucumber in a bowl and toss with the fresh lemon juice and chili powder.
2. Plate and serve right away.

Serving Suggestion: Serve with lemon wedges on the side.
Variation Tip: Feel free to add more seasoning.
Nutritional Information per Serving:
Calories 88 | Fat 0.9g | Sodium 46mg | Carbs 20.2g | Fiber 9.8g | Sugar 4.7g | Protein 2.2g

Garlic Hummus

Prep Time: 10 Minutes
Cook Time: 0 Minutes
Serves: 2

Ingredients:
- ½ teaspoon salt
- ¼ cup tahini
- 1 can no-salt-added chickpeas
- ¼ cup olive oil
- ½ teaspoon chili powder
- 1 clove garlic, peeled
- ¼ cup lemon juice
- 1 teaspoon ground cumin

Preparation:

1. Add all the ingredients, including the chickpea liquid, to a blender and blend until smooth.
2. Scrape off the container edges and keep blending until all the ingredients are well combined.
3. Serve with extra olive oil drizzled on top.
Serving Suggestion: Serve with pita chips.
Variation Tip: Add cayenne pepper for a hotter flavor.
Nutritional Information per Serving:
Calories 152 | Fat 11.9g | Sodium 336mg | Carbs 9.7g | Fiber 4.6g | Sugar 0.2g | Protein 3.7g

Asian Green Triangles

Prep Time: 15 minutes
Cook Time: 10 minutes
Servings: 3

Ingredients:
- ½ cup low-fat ricotta
- ½ tablespoon fresh basil, chopped
- 3 sheets filo pastry
- ½ brown onion, finely diced
- ½ teaspoon low-sodium soy sauce
- ½ bunch baby bok choy, thinly sliced
- ½ garlic clove, crushed

Preparation:
1. Preheat the oven to 360°F and lightly grease a baking sheet.
2. In a bowl, mix the onion, bok choy, garlic, soy sauce, basil, and ricotta cheese until well combined.
3. Position one sheet of filo pastry on a clean, flat surface and fold it in thirds lengthwise.
4. Spread some of the onion mixture onto the pastry strip's top.
5. Fold the strip to form a triangle.
6. Place the triangle onto the prepared baking sheet. Repeat for the rest of the filo pastry and onion mixture. Lightly spray the triangles with cooking spray.
7. Bake in the preheated oven for about 10 minutes or until golden brown.
Serving Suggestions: You can serve with a dipping sauce of your choice.
Variation Tip: You can use low-fat cottage cheese instead of ricotta.
Nutritional Information per Serving:
Calories: 66|Fat: 3.3g|Sat Fat: 2g|Carbohydrates: 4.2g|Fiber: 0.5g|Sugar: 1.1g|Protein: 5.2g

Paprika Roasted Pecans

Prep Time: 10 Minutes
Cook Time: 12 Minutes
Serves: 1
Ingredients:
• 2 tablespoons pecan halves
• ½ teaspoon extra-virgin olive oil
• ⅛ teaspoon fresh rosemary, chopped
• Pinch of smoked paprika
• Pinch of cayenne pepper
• Pinch of salt
Preparation:
1. Preheat the oven to 350°F. Line a baking sheet with parchment paper.
2. Thoroughly mix all of the ingredients in a bowl.
3. Place the coated pecans on the prepared baking sheet.
4. Cook for 10–12 minutes in the preheated oven, flipping twice during cooking.
5. Remove the baking sheet from the oven and set it aside to cool.
6. Serve and enjoy.
Serving Suggestion: Toss the pecans into salads.
Variation Tip: Substitute pecans with walnuts.
Nutritional Information per Serving:
Calories 126| Fat 8.1g | Sodium 156mg | Carbs 2.5g | Fiber 1.8g | Sugar 0.6g | Protein 1.6g

Pistachio and Apricot Chicken Patties

Prep Time: 25 minutes
Cook Time: 10 minutes
Servings: 2
Ingredients:
• ½ cup dried apricots
• 2 tablespoons pistachio nuts
• 1-pound chicken, minced
• 2 slices multi-grain bread
• ½ teaspoon cracked black pepper
Preparation:
1. Line a baking sheet with parchment paper.
2. Add the apricots, chicken, bread, and pistachios to a bowl and season with the cracked black pepper. Mix well.
3. Shape the mixture into patties and space out evenly onto the prepared baking sheet. Allow the patties to chill for 20 minutes.
4. Grease a non-stick skillet over medium heat. Add the patties and cook them on each side for 4 to 5 minutes or until golden and cooked through.
Serving Suggestions: Serve topped with fresh parsley.
Variation Tip: You can also add almonds to this recipe.
Nutritional Information per Serving:
Calories: 450|Fat: 10g|Sat Fat: 2.4g|Carbohydrates: 16.5g|Fiber: 3.1g|Sugar: 5.4g|Protein: 70.5g

Cobb Salad

Prep Time: 10 minutes
Cook Time: 0 minutes
Servings: 4
Ingredients:
• 4 ounces chicken breast, shredded
• 4 cups mixed green salad
• 2 ounces feta cheese, crumbled
• 8 cherry tomatoes, diced
• 2 hardboiled eggs, diced
• ½ cup cooked bacon, crumbled
• 1 avocado, diced
Preparation:
1. Mix the tomatoes, avocado, and eggs in a large bowl with the green salad.
2. Top the salad with the feta cheese, shredded chicken breast, and crumbled bacon.
3. Serve and enjoy!
Serving Suggestions: Serve drizzled with a splash of olive oil.
Variation Tip: You can use goat's cheese instead of feta.
Nutritional Information per Serving:
Calories: 268|Fat: 17.2g|Sat Fat: 5.3g|Carbohydrates: 16.2g|Fiber: 6.8g|Sugar: 7.5g|Protein: 15.3g

Air Fryer Plantain Chips

Prep Time: 10 minutes
Cook Time: 14 minutes
Servings: 2
Ingredients:
• Avocado oil spray
• 1 green plantain, peeled and cut into strips
• Pinch of salt
Preparation:
1. Preheat an air fryer to 350°F.
2. Spray the air fryer basket with avocado oil.
3. Arrange the plantain strips in a single layer in the basket and spray them with avocado oil.
4. Cook for about 14 minutes, flipping halfway through the cooking time.
5. Season with salt and serve.
Serving Suggestions: Serve with sugar-free salsa.
Variation Tip: You can use an olive oil spray instead.
Nutritional Information per Serving:
Calories: 109|Fat: 0.3g|Sat Fat: 0.1g|Carbohydrates: 28.5g|Fiber: 2.1g|Sugar: 13.4g|Protein: 1.2g

Mexican Jicama Snack

Prep Time: 10 minutes
Cook Time: 0 minutes
Servings: 6

Ingredients:
• 2 limes, juiced
• 1 large jicama, peeled and cut into French fry-sized sticks
• 1 tablespoon cayenne pepper
Preparation:
1. Mix the jicama sticks with the lime juice and cayenne pepper in a medium bowl and toss well.
2. Serve as finger food.
Serving Suggestions: Sprinkle with nigella seeds and fresh coriander before serving.
Variation Tip: You can also use lemon juice instead of lime.
Nutritional Information per Serving:
Calories: 83.9|Fat: 0.4g|Sat Fat: 0.1g|Carbohydrates: 19.6g|Fiber: 10.3g|Sugar: 4g|Protein: 1.7g

Chicken Nuggets

Prep Time: 20 minutes
Cook Time: 24 minutes
Servings: 4
Ingredients:
• 4 tablespoons extra-virgin olive oil
• 2 tablespoons Italian seasoning
• Salt and black pepper, to taste
• 1 cup almond flour
• 4 boneless, skinless chicken breasts, cut into chunks
Preparation:
1. Preheat the oven to 400°F and lightly grease a baking sheet.
2. Combine the Italian seasoning, almond flour, salt, and black pepper in a bowl. Mix well.
3. Brush the chicken chunks with olive oil and dredge in the flour mixture.
4. Put the chicken pieces onto the baking sheet and bake for about 20 minutes in the preheated oven.
5. Turn on the broiler and place the cooked chicken under it for 4 minutes for crispiness.
6. Dish out and serve immediately.
Serving Suggestions: Serve with homemade sugar-free ketchup.
Variation Tip: You can also use coconut flour.
Nutritional Information per Serving:
Calories: 576|Fat: 39.8g|Sat Fat: 6.2g|Carbohydrates: 6.8g|Fiber: 3g|Sugar: 0.6g|Protein: 46.5g

Grilled Veggie Wrap

Prep Time: 7 minutes
Cook Time: 8 minutes
Servings: 2
Ingredients:

- 2 large low-carb, whole-wheat tortillas
- ½ red bell pepper, sliced into 4 slices
- ¼ cup hummus
- ½ tablespoon olive oil
- ¼ teaspoon black pepper
- ½ yellow squash, sliced lengthwise
- 4 fresh basil leaves
- 1 tablespoon balsamic vinegar
- ½ zucchini, sliced lengthwise

Preparation:
1. Preheat the broiler.
2. Combine the olive oil, balsamic vinegar, and black pepper in a large bowl. Whisk well.
3. Add the squash, zucchini, and bell pepper to the bowl and keep aside for 5 minutes.
4. Place the marinated veggies onto a baking sheet and under the broiler. Broil for about 3 minutes on both sides.
5. Layer the hummus on the tortillas and top with the basil leaves and veggies.
6. Roll the tortillas up like burritos before serving.

Serving Suggestions: Serve with your choice of low-carb dip.
Variation Tip: You can also use apple cider vinegar.
Nutritional Information per Serving:
Calories: 222|Fat: 7.7g|Sat Fat: 1g|Carbohydrates: 32.1g|Fiber: 6.4g|Sugar: 2.9g|Protein: 7.9g

Pork Tenderloin with Apple-Onion Chutney

Prep Time: 10 minutes
Cook Time: 18 minutes
Servings: 2

Ingredients:
- ⅛ teaspoon dried thyme, crushed
- ¾ cup onion, thinly sliced
- 1 (8-ounce) piece pork tenderloin, fat trimmed and cut in half crosswise
- ¼ teaspoon black pepper
- 8 ounces apple, cored and sliced
- 2 tablespoons cider vinegar
- ¼ teaspoon salt
- 1 sprig fresh thyme, chopped
- ¼ cup water
- 1 teaspoon honey
- ⅛ teaspoon ground cumin

Preparation:
1. Place each pork piece, cut side down, between two plastic wrap pieces, and pound them to ½-inch thickness with a meat mallet.
2. Discard the plastic wrap and season the meat with the dried thyme and pepper.
3. Lightly coat a skillet with cooking spray and add the pork.
4. Cook for about 9 minutes over medium-high heat, turning once in between.
5. Dish out the pork onto a plate and cover to keep warm.
6. For the chutney: Cook the onions for about 4 minutes in the same skillet, occasionally stirring.
7. Stir in the apple slices, vinegar, water, salt, honey, and cumin. Let it reach a boil, then reduce the heat. Simmer for about 5 minutes, occasionally stirring.
8. Put the pork back into the skillet and heat it through.
9. Dish out the pork and chutney onto plates to serve.

Serving Suggestions: Serve garnished with fresh thyme.
Variation Tip: You can use any variety of apples.
Nutritional Information per Serving:
Calories: 219|Fat: 2.4g|Sat Fat: 0.8g|Carbohydrates: 24.5g|Fiber: 3.8g|Sugar: 17.3g|Protein: 24.7g

Spicy Lamb Casserole

Prep Time: 10 Minutes
Cook Time: 2 Hours 15 Minutes
Serves: 4

Ingredients:
- 2 tablespoons canola oil
- 1½ pounds lamb shoulder, cut into chunks
- ½ sweet onion, finely chopped
- 1 tablespoon ginger, grated
- 2 teaspoons garlic, minced
- 1 teaspoon ground cinnamon
- 1 teaspoon ground cumin
- ¼ teaspoon ground cloves
- 2 white sweet potatoes, peeled and diced
- 2 cups low-sodium beef broth
- Fine Himalayan pink salt, to taste
- Black pepper, to taste
- 2 teaspoons parsley, chopped, for garnish
- 2 teaspoons mint, finely chopped, for garnish

Preparation:
1. Preheat the oven to 300°F
2. Place a pan over medium-high heat and add the canola oil.
3. Add the lamb chunks and fry for 6 minutes until browned, stirring occasionally.
4. Add the chopped onion, grated ginger, minced garlic, ground cinnamon, ground cumin, and ground cloves, and fry for 5 minutes.
5. Add the diced sweet potatoes and low-sodium beef broth and bring the stew to a boil.
6. Transfer the lamb mixture into an ovenproof casserole dish, cover with a lid or aluminum foil, and place into the preheated oven.
7. Cook for 2 hours, occasionally stirring, until the lamb is tender.
8. Remove the stew from the oven and season with fine Himalayan pink salt and ground black pepper.
Serving Suggestion: Garnish with the chopped parsley and mint.
Variation Tip: Substitute beef broth with a broth of your choice.
Nutritional Information per Serving:
Calories 503 | Fat 27.6g | Sodium 640mg | Carbs 15.6g | Fiber 3g | Sugar 4.5g | Protein 45.8g

Grilled Lamb Racks

Prep Time: 2 Hours 10 Minutes
Cook Time: 20 Minutes
Serves: 4

Ingredients:
• 1 tablespoon olive oil
• 1 tablespoon garlic, minced
• Salt and black pepper, to taste
• 2 (1-inch) sprig fresh rosemary
• 2 (1½ pounds) French lamb racks, trimmed of fat, cut into 4 pieces with 2 bones, leaving 1 bone with an equal amount of meat

Preparation:
1. Combine all the ingredients in a large bowl. Toss to coat the lamb racks well.
2. Wrap the bowl in plastic and refrigerate to marinate for at least 2 hours.
3. Preheat the broiler on medium heat and grease a sheet pan with olive oil.
4. Remove the bowl from the refrigerator, and arrange the lamb racks on the sheet pan, bone side down.
5. Place the sheet pan 8 inches from the heat source (the third rack down) and broil the lamb for about 10 minutes or until it reaches your desired doneness. Flip the lamb halfway through the cooking time.
6. Remove the lamb racks and serve hot.

Serving Suggestion: Garnish with rosemary sprigs.
Variation Tip: Feel free to add more seasoning.
Nutritional Information per Serving:
Calories 192 | Fat 9g | Sodium 211mg | Carbs 1g | Fiber 0g | Sugar 0g | Protein 22g

Butter-Glazed Lamb Chops

Prep Time: 10 Minutes
Cook Time: 5 Minutes
Serves: 4

Ingredients:
• 4 lamb chops
• 1 teaspoon rosemary, diced
• 1 tablespoon unsalted butter
• Salt and black pepper, to taste

Preparation:
1. Season the lamb chops with salt and pepper.
2. Place the lamb in a single layer in the air fryer basket and place the basket into the air fryer.
3. Seal with the air fryer lid, select "Air Fry" mode, then set the cooking temperature to 400 ℉ and timer for 5 minutes.
4. Meanwhile, mix the butter and rosemary. Spread the mixture over the air-fried lamb chops.
5. Serve hot.

Serving Suggestion: Serve with your favorite greens.
Variation Tip: Add smoked paprika for a varied flavor.
Nutritional Information per Serving:
Calories 278 | Fat 12.8g | Sodium 183mg | Carbs 0.2g | Fiber 2g | Sugar 1g | Protein 38g

Lamb Chops with Lime

Prep Time: 4 Hours 10 Minutes
Cook Time: 10 Minutes
Serves: 4

Ingredients:
• ¼ cup olive oil
• ¼ cup lime juice
• 2 tablespoons lime zest
• 2 tablespoons mint, chopped
• 2 tablespoons parsley, chopped
• Pinch of Himalayan pink salt
• Black pepper, to taste
• 12 lamb chops

Preparation:
1. Combine the olive oil, lime juice, lime zest, chopped parsley, chopped mint, ground Himalayan pink salt, and ground black pepper in a small mixing dish.
2. Pour the mixture into a lidded marinating dish and add the lamb chops. Stir well to blend everything together.
3. Cover the marinating dish with the lid and refrigerate for 4 hours, flipping it over many times.
4. Preheat the broiler over medium heat.
5. Remove the chops from the dish and place them on a baking sheet lined with aluminum foil.
6. Remove the rest of the marinade and discard it.
7. Cook the lamb chops on the third rack for around 4 minutes on each side or until the desired doneness. Before serving, let the lamb chops rest for 5 minutes.

Serving Suggestion: Serve with lemon wedges.
Variation Tip: You may thicken the remaining marinade by cooking it down.
Nutritional Information per Serving:
Calories 413 | Fat 29g | Sodium 302mg | Carbs 1g | Fiber 0.6g | Sugar 0.3g | Protein 31g

Mustard Pork Chops

Prep Time: 10 Minutes
Cook Time: 25 Minutes
Serves: 4

Ingredients:
- ¼ cup Dijon mustard
- 1 tablespoon pure maple syrup
- 2 tablespoons rice vinegar
- 4 bone-in, thin-cut pork chops

Preparation:
1. Preheat the oven to 400ºF.
2. Combine the mustard, maple syrup, and rice vinegar in a small saucepan. Stir to mix and bring to a simmer over medium heat.
3. Cook for about 2 minutes until just slightly thickened.
4. Place the pork chops in a baking dish and spoon the sauce over them, flipping to coat.
5. Bake, uncovered, for 18–22 minutes in the preheated oven until the juices run clear.

Serving Suggestion: Garnish with rosemary sprigs.
Variation Tip: Substitute rice vinegar with apple cider vinegar.
Nutritional Information per Serving:
Calories 258 | Fat 10.6g | Sodium 238mg | Carbs 4.2g | Fiber 0.5g | Sugar 3.1g | Protein 23.7g

Tangy Pork Chops

Prep Time: 10 Minutes
Cook Time: 10 Minutes
Serves: 2

Ingredients:
- 2 boneless pork chops
- 2 tablespoons canola oil
- ½ ounce packed dark brown sugar
- ½ teaspoon Hungarian paprika
- ½ teaspoon ground mustard
- ½ teaspoon onion powder
- ½ teaspoon garlic powder
- Salt and black pepper, to taste

Preparation:

1. Preheat the air fryer for 5 minutes at 350℉.
2. Cover the pork chops with oil.
3. Mix all the spices and season the pork chops abundantly with the mixture, almost as if you were breading them.
4. Place the pork chops in the air fryer basket. Set the cooking time to 10 minutes. Flip the chops halfway through the cooking time.
5. Remove the pork chops and let them stand for a few minutes before serving.

Serving Suggestion: Serve with asparagus.
Variation Tip: Replace canola oil with olive oil.
Nutritional Information per Serving:
Calories 118 | Fat 12g | Sodium 346mg | Carbs 0.3g | Fiber 3g | Sugar 6g | Protein 13.1g

Pork Piccata

Prep Time: 10 Minutes
Cook Time: 15 Minutes
Serves: 4

Ingredients:
- ½ cup almond flour
- ½ teaspoon garlic powder
- ¼ teaspoon sea salt
- ¼ teaspoon freshly ground black pepper
- 4 (4-ounce) boneless pork chops, pounded flat
- 2 teaspoons olive oil
- ½ cup low-sodium chicken broth
- Juice and zest of 1 lemon, divided
- 2 tablespoons capers
- 1 tablespoon fresh parsley, chopped

Preparation:
1. Combine the flour, garlic powder, salt, and pepper in a small bowl.
2. Dredge the pork chops in the flour mixture, shaking off any excess.
3. In a large skillet, heat the oil over medium-high heat.
4. Cook the pork, turning once, until browned and just cooked through, about 10 minutes.
5. Transfer the pork to a plate and set it aside.
6. Add the broth to the skillet, scraping up any browned bits.
7. Add the lemon juice, reduce the heat to low, and simmer for about 2 minutes, until it's reduced by half.
8. Add the lemon zest, capers, and parsley.
9. Serve hot.

Serving Suggestion: Serve the pork cutlets with the lemon-caper sauce.
Variation Tip: Piccata means "to pound flat" in Italian, and you can do that here with a mallet or rolling pin or buy the pork pre-pounded.
Nutritional Information per Serving:
Calories 220 | Fat 7g | Sodium 303mg | Carbs 12g | Fiber 2g | Sugar 0g | Protein 28g

Curry Pork Chops

Prep Time: 10 Minutes
Cook Time: 25 Minutes
Serves: 2

Ingredients:
- 2 pork loin chops
- 1 teaspoon curry powder
- ¼ cup soy milk
- 1 onion, diced
- 1 tablespoon olive oil

Preparation:
1. Heat the olive oil in a non-stick skillet.
2. Add the pork chops and cook them for 5 minutes per side. Remove the pork chops and add the diced onion to the skillet.
3. Cook the onion for 4 minutes or until tender.
4. Add the curry powder and soy milk. Bring the mixture to a boil.
5. Add the cooked pork chops and coat them well in the curry mixture.
6. Close the lid and simmer for 10 minutes on low heat.

Serving Suggestion: Garnish with chopped green onions.
Variation Tip: Substitute soy milk with your favorite nut milk.

Nutritional Information per Serving:
Calories 358 | Fat 27.6g | Sodium 74mg | Carbs 7.6g | Fiber 1.7g | Sugar 3.6g | Protein 19.7g

Pork Roast with Orange Sauce

Prep Time: 10 Minutes
Cook Time: 1 Hour 18 Minutes
Serves: 4

Ingredients:
- 1-pound pork loin roast
- ½ cup carrot, diced
- ½ cup celery stalk, chopped
- ½ cup onion, diced
- 1 teaspoon Italian seasonings
- 1 cup orange juice
- 1 tablespoon potato starch

Preparation:
1. Preheat the oven to 365℉.

2. Rub the pork loin roast with the Italian seasonings.
3. Put the carrot, celery stalk, and diced onion in a roasting pan. Put the meat over the vegetables. Add the orange juice.
4. Bake in the preheated oven for 75 minutes.
5. Transfer all the vegetables and juices from the pan to a large saucepan. Bring the mixture to a boil over medium-high heat.
6. Blend the mixture with the help of the blender. Add the potato starch and whisk well.
7. Return to the saucepan and simmer the sauce for 3 minutes.
8. Slice the cooked meat and drizzle the sauce over it.

Serving Suggestion: Garnish with orange slices.
Variation Tip: Substitute orange juice with lemon juice.

Nutritional Information per Serving:
Calories 292 | Fat 11.4g | Sodium 87mg | Carbs 12.2g | Fiber 1g | Sugar 6.8g | Protein 33.2g

Healthy Oven-Fried Pork Chops

Prep Time: 15 minutes
Cook Time: 20 minutes
Servings: 4

Ingredients:
- ¼ cup all-purpose flour
- 1 teaspoon Dijon mustard
- 1 teaspoon ground pepper
- 4 (4-ounce each) boneless pork chops, ¾-inch-thick
- Cooking spray
- 1 large egg, lightly beaten
- ¾ cup whole-wheat panko breadcrumbs
- ½ teaspoon kosher salt

Preparation:
1. Preheat the oven to 400°F and lightly grease a baking sheet.
2. Place the flour in a shallow dish.
3. Whisk the beaten egg and mustard in another dish.
4. Mix the panko and pepper in a third shallow dish.
5. Season both sides of the pork chops with salt.
6. Dredge the pork chops in the flour, coat in the egg mixture, then cover with the panko.
7. Place the pork chops on the baking sheet and bake for about 20 minutes in the preheated oven.
8. Dish out onto a platter and serve.

Serving Suggestions: Serve with sautéed veggies.
Variation Tip: You can also use almond or coconut flour.

Nutritional Information per Serving:
Calories: 194|Fat: 6.3g|Sat Fat: 1.8g|Carbohydrates: 11.7g|Fiber: 1.7g|Sugar: 0.4g|Protein: 21.9g

Sirloin Steak

Prep Time: 10 Minutes
Cook Time: 30 Minutes
Serves: 4

Ingredients:
• 1 (1-pound) boneless beef top sirloin steak, 1–1½ inches thick, trimmed of all visible fat
• ¼ teaspoon salt
• ⅛ teaspoon pepper
• 2 teaspoons canola oil
• Lemon wedges, for garnish

Preparation:
1. Pat the steak dry with paper towels and sprinkle with salt and pepper.
2. Heat the oil in a 12-inch skillet over medium-high heat until just smoking.
3. Add the steak and brown it well on each side, 3–5 minutes.
4. Flip the steak and continue to cook until the meat registers 125°F (for medium-rare), 5–10 minutes, reducing the heat as needed to prevent scorching.
5. Transfer the steak to a carving board, tent it with aluminum foil, and let it rest for 5 minutes.
6. Slice the steak thin and serve.

Serving Suggestion: Serve with lemon wedges.
Variation Tip: Feel free to add more seasonings.
Nutritional Information per Serving:
Calories 233 | Fat 9.4g | Sodium 222mg | Carbs 0.5g | Fiber 0.2g | Sugar 0g | Protein 25g

Beef Fajitas

Prep Time: 7 minutes
Cook Time: 5 minutes
Servings: 6

Ingredients:
• ½ teaspoon cilantro, freshly chopped
• ½ teaspoon lime juice
• 2 avocados
• 1 teaspoon chili powder
• 2 pounds beef, cut into strips
• 2 red bell peppers, seeded and cut into strips
• Salt, to taste

• 1 teaspoon cumin
• ½ tablespoon olive oil
• 2 red onions, sliced
• 2 yellow bell peppers, seeded and cut into strips

Preparation:
1. Season the beef strips with salt and black pepper.
2. Put the olive oil in a cast-iron skillet and cook the seasoned beef strips for about 1 minute per side over medium heat.
3. Take out the beef strips, place them on a warm serving plate, and keep them aside.
4. Add the onions and bell peppers to the skillet along with the cumin and chili powder.
5. Stir-fry for about 3 minutes, then add to the beef.
6. Squeeze with lemon juice before serving.

Serving Suggestions: Serve garnished with fresh coriander and sliced avocado.
Variation Tip: You can also make chicken fajitas with this recipe.
Nutritional Information per Serving:
Calories: 400|Fat: 22.5g|Sat Fat: 5.6g|Carbohydrates: 14.9g|Fiber: 6.7g|Sugar: 5.3g|Protein: 36g

Marinated Steak and Broccoli

Prep Time: 5 minutes (plus 1 hour for marinating)
Cook Time: 5 minutes
Serving: 2

Ingredients:
• 8 ounces broccoli, cut into small florets
• 8 ounces lean beef, sliced into ½-inch thick strips
• 2 teaspoons soy sauce
• 2 teaspoons olive oil
• 2 teaspoons balsamic vinegar
• Pinch of pepper

Preparation:
1. Mix the soy sauce, balsamic vinegar, olive oil, and pepper in a bowl.
2. Add the beef strips and refrigerate for 1 hour.
3. Put the olive oil in a pan and fry the steak and broccoli for about 5 minutes over medium-high heat.
4. Remove from the heat and serve right away.

Serving Suggestions: Serve over rice.
Variation Tip: You can also use coconut aminos instead of soy sauce.
Nutritional Information per Serving:
Calories: 309|Fat: 16.9g|Sat Fat: 5.6g|Carbohydrates: 12.7g|Fiber: 3.1g|Sugar: 3.7g|Protein: 27.3g

Paprika Baked Pork Tenderloin with Potatoes and Broccoli

Prep Time: 20 minutes
Cook Time: 40 minutes
Servings: 4
Ingredients:
- ¾ teaspoon salt, divided
- 2 tablespoons olive oil, divided
- 1½ teaspoons smoked paprika
- 1 red onion, cut into 1-inch pieces
- ¾ pound Yukon Gold potatoes, scrubbed and cut into 1-inch pieces
- 4 cups broccoli florets
- 2 teaspoons Dijon mustard
- 1 teaspoon lemon juiced
- 1 (1-pound) pork tenderloin, trimmed
- 2 jarred roasted red bell peppers
- 2 cloves garlic, peeled
- ½ teaspoon ground pepper, divided
- 2 tablespoons low-fat sour cream

Preparation:
1. Preheat the oven to 425°F and grease a baking sheet with cooking spray. Mix the potatoes, onion, 1 tablespoon of olive oil, and ¼ teaspoon of salt in a medium bowl; toss well.
2. Spread the potato mixture onto the baking sheet and roast in the preheated oven for 15 minutes.
3. Meanwhile, mix the broccoli, 2 teaspoons of olive oil, and ¼ teaspoon of salt in a medium bowl; toss well.
4. Put the garlic on a piece of foil, drizzle over the remaining 1 teaspoon of olive oil, then wrap it up.
5. Mix the paprika, ¼ teaspoon of ground pepper, and the remaining ¼ teaspoon of salt in a bowl.
6. Rub the mustard all over the pork and coat it with the paprika mixture. Place it onto a greased baking sheet.
7. Remove the potatoes from the oven and place them with the pork along with the broccoli and wrapped garlic.
8. Place in the oven and roast for about 25 minutes, then set aside. Allow the pork to rest before cutting it into slices.
9. Unwrap the garlic and put it in a blender along with the roasted red peppers, sour cream, lemon juice, and remaining ¼ teaspoon of ground pepper. Blend well.
Serving Suggestions: Serve the pork with the potatoes and veggies and drizzle over the red pepper sauce.
Variation Tip: You can add any veggies you prefer.

Nutritional Information per Serving:
Calories: 323|Fat: 10.3g|Sat Fat: 2.1g|Carbohydrates: 28.7g|Fiber: 5.3g|Sugar: 5.5g|Protein: 30g

Baked Cavatelli Casserole

Prep Time: 15 minutes
Cook Time: 1 hour
Servings: 8
Ingredients:
- 12 ounces ground Italian sausage, uncooked
- 1 cup fresh cremini mushrooms, chopped
- 1 medium onion, chopped
- 1 (14½-ounce) can no-salt-added diced tomatoes, undrained
- 1 tablespoon dried basil, crushed
- ¼ teaspoon salt
- 4 ounces reduced-fat Italian blend cheese, shredded
- 8 ounces dried cavatelli
- 1 cup zucchini, chopped
- 1 medium red sweet pepper, chopped
- 2 garlic cloves, minced
- 1 (8-ounce) can no-salt-added tomato sauce
- 1 teaspoon dried oregano, crushed
- ¼ teaspoon black pepper

Preparation:
1. Preheat the oven to 350°F and grease a baking dish with olive oil.
2. Cook the cavatelli according to the directions.
3. Meanwhile, in a large skillet, cook the sausage, mushrooms, eggplant, sweet pepper, garlic, and onions over medium heat for about 5 minutes.
4. Add the tomato sauce, tomatoes, dried oregano, basil, salt, and black pepper. Let it reach a boil, then reduce the heat to low.
5. Secure the lid and simmer for 10 minutes, occasionally stirring the mixture.
6. Stir in the fresh basil and oregano.
7. In a large bowl, mix the pasta and sausage mixture. Pour the mixture into the prepared baking dish, cover it, and bake in the preheated oven for about 40 minutes.
8. Uncover, top with the cheese, and bake for another 5 minutes.
Serving Suggestions: Serve sprinkled with feta cheese.
Variation Tip: You can also use Italian turkey sausage.
Nutritional Information per Serving:
Calories: 254|Fat: 7.1g|Sat Fat: 2.7g|Carbohydrates: 30.1g|Fiber: 3.2g|Sugar: 5.5g|Protein: 16.8g

Ground Beef and Zucchini Lasagna

Prep Time: 20 minutes
Cook Time: 1 hour 17 minutes
Servings: 4

Ingredients:
- 1 cup low-fat mozzarella, shredded
- 2 teaspoons dried thyme
- 1 cube chicken bouillon
- 2 teaspoons paprika
- 2 teaspoons dried basil
- 4 zucchinis, sliced
- 4 cloves garlic, chopped
- 6 tomatoes, ends cut off
- Salt and black pepper, to taste
- 32 ounces ground beef
- 9 ounces onion, chopped
- 2 Serrano chilies, chopped
- 11 ounces mushrooms, chopped

Preparation:
1. Preheat the oven to 375°F and lightly grease a baking dish.
2. Season the zucchini slices with salt and then blot them with a paper towel. Grill the zucchini slices in a grill pan for 3 minutes on high heat and then remove from the heat.
3. Meanwhile, place the cut tomatoes in a pan of boiling water for a few minutes. Remove the tomatoes, rinse them with cold water, then peel off their skin.
4. Spray a deep skillet with a little cooking spray and fry the garlic, onion, and chili for about 1 minute. Add the tomatoes and mushrooms to the skillet and sauté for about 4 minutes. Remove the mixture from the skillet and set it aside.
5. Brown the beef in the same skillet with the paprika.
6. Return the vegetables to the skillet with the chicken bouillon and remaining spices. Simmer for 25 minutes over low heat.
7. Place a layer of zucchini slices in the prepared baking dish and top with the meat sauce. Add another layer of zucchini, then a layer of meat sauce. Continue layering until all the ingredients have been used.
8. Sprinkle mozzarella on top and bake in the preheated oven for about 35 minutes.

9. Remove the lasagna from the oven and set it aside for about 10 minutes before serving.
Serving Suggestions: Serve topped with arugula.
Variation Tip: You can also use ground pork or lamb.
Nutritional Information per Serving:
Calories: 552|Fat: 15.5g|Sat Fat: 5.5g|Carbohydrates: 25.1g|Fiber: 7.4g|Sugar: 12.9g|Protein: 78.5g

Braised Beef with Carrots and Turnips

Prep Time: 10 minutes
Cook Time: 8 hours 12 minutes
Servings: 10

Ingredients:
- 2 teaspoons ground cinnamon
- ½ teaspoon ground pepper
- 1 tablespoon kosher salt
- ½ teaspoon ground allspice
- ¼ teaspoon ground cloves
- 2 tablespoons extra-virgin olive oil
- 3 cloves garlic, sliced
- 1 (28-ounce) can whole tomatoes
- 2 medium turnips, peeled and cut into ½-inch pieces
- 3 pounds beef chuck roast, trimmed
- 1 medium onion, chopped
- 1 cup red wine
- 5 medium carrots, cut into 1-inch pieces

Preparation:
1. Mix the salt, cinnamon, allspice, pepper, and cloves in a bowl.
2. Rub the spice mixture all over the beef.
3. Put the olive oil in a large skillet and cook the beef for about 5 minutes per side over medium heat.
4. Transfer the beef to a slow cooker.
5. Add the onion and garlic to the skillet and cook for about 2 minutes.
6. Drizzle in the wine and tomatoes and let it reach a boil, stirring to combine.
7. Transfer the mixture into the slow cooker over the beef and add the carrots and turnips.
8. Secure the lid and cook on low pressure for 8 hours.
9. Remove the beef from the slow cooker and slice. Serve the beef with the veggies and sauce.
Serving Suggestions: Serve over cooked rice.
Variation Tip: You can use parsnips instead of turnips.
Nutritional Information per Serving:
Calories: 579|Fat: 40.9g|Sat Fat: 15.5g|Carbohydrates: 10.2g|Fiber: 2.7g|Sugar: 5.3g|Protein: 37g

Honey-Baked Lamb Ribs

Prep Time: 15 Minutes
Cook Time: 30 Minutes
Serves: 3

Ingredients:
• 10 ounces lamb ribs, trimmed
• 1 tablespoon canola oil
• 1 tablespoon lemon juice
• 1 teaspoon liquid honey

Preparation:
1. Preheat the oven to 355℉. Lightly grease a baking sheet with cooking oil.
2. Mix the canola oil with the lemon juice and honey.
3. Brush the lamb ribs with the sweet mixture and leave to marinate for 15 minutes.
4. Place the marinated ribs on the baking sheet and bake them for 30 minutes in the preheated oven.
5. Flip the lamb ribs halfway through the cooking time.

Serving Suggestion: Garnish with rosemary sprigs.
Variation Tip: Substitute honey with maple syrup.
Nutritional Information per Serving:
Calories 269 | Fat 17.3g | Sodium 78mg | Carbs 2g | Fiber 0g | Sugar 2g | Protein 24.8g

Lamb Cutlets

Prep Time: 4 Hours 10 Minutes
Cook Time: 8 Minutes
Serves: 4

Ingredients:
• ¼ cup freshly squeezed lime juice
• 2 tablespoons lime zest
• 2 tablespoons fresh parsley, chopped
• Sea salt and black pepper, to taste
• 1 tablespoon extra-virgin olive oil
• 12 lamb cutlets (about 1½ pounds)

Preparation:
1. Combine the lime juice and zest, parsley, salt, black pepper, and olive oil in a large bowl. Stir to mix well.

2. Dunk the lamb cutlets in the lime mixture, then toss to coat well. Wrap the bowl in plastic and refrigerate to marinate for at least 4 hours.
3. Preheat the oven to 450ºF. Line a baking sheet with aluminum foil.
4. Remove the bowl from the refrigerator, let it sit for 10 minutes, then discard the marinade.
5. Arrange the lamb cutlets on the baking sheet.
6. Bake the lamb in the preheated oven for 8 minutes or until it reaches your desired doneness. Flip the cutlets halfway through the cooking time with tongs to make sure they are cooked evenly.
7. Serve immediately.

Serving Suggestion: Serve with roasted vegetables.
Variation Tip: Substitute lime with lemon.
Nutritional Information per Serving:
Calories 297 | Fat 18g | Sodium 389mg | Carbs 1g | Fiber 0g | Sugar 0g | Protein 31g

Beef Bulgogi

Prep Time: 15 minutes (plus overnight for marinating)
Cook Time: 4 minutes
Servings: 4

Ingredients:
• ¼ cup green onion, chopped
• 5 tablespoons soy sauce
• 2 tablespoons sesame seeds
• 1 teaspoon Splenda
• 2 tablespoons sesame oil
• 1 pound flank steak, thinly sliced
• 2 tablespoons garlic, minced
• ½ teaspoon black pepper

Preparation:
1. Combine the soy sauce, green onion, sugar, garlic, sesame oil, sesame seeds, and black pepper in a small bowl.
2. Put the beef in a shallow dish and drizzle the soy sauce mixture over it.
3. Cover the dish and refrigerate overnight.
4. Lightly grease a grill pan and heat it up over medium-high heat.
5. Add the marinated beef and cook for about 2 minutes per side, until slightly charred.

Serving Suggestions: Top with sesame seeds and green onions to serve over basmati rice.
Variation Tip: You can also use stevia instead of Splenda.
Nutritional Information per Serving:
Calories: 330|Fat: 18.5g|Sat Fat: 5.2g|Carbohydrates: 5.6g|Fiber: 1g|Sugar: 1.5g|Protein: 34g

Ginger Beef Stir-Fry with Peppers

Prep Time: 20 minutes
Cook Time: 12 minutes
Servings: 4
Ingredients:
• 12 ounces lean flank steak, trimmed into 2-inch-wide strips
• 1 tablespoon reduced-sodium soy sauce, divided
• 1 teaspoon vegetable oil plus 1 tablespoon, divided
• 4 teaspoons ketchup
• 3 slices ginger, peeled and smashed
• 1 cup green bell pepper, diced into 1-inch pieces
• 2 tablespoons beef broth, unsalted
• 1½ teaspoons cornstarch
• 1 teaspoon dry sherry plus 1 tablespoon, divided
• 4 teaspoons hoisin sauce
• 3 teaspoons chili-garlic sauce
• 1 small yellow onion, thinly sliced
• 1 tablespoon olive oil
• 1 cup red bell pepper, diced
Preparation:
1. Mix the beef, cornstarch, 1½ teaspoons of soy sauce, and 1 teaspoon of sherry in a bowl. Mix thoroughly.
2. Put 1 teaspoon of olive oil in a wok and cook the beef over medium-high heat for about 3 minutes per side. Remove the beef.
3. Mix the hoisin sauce, ketchup, chili-garlic sauce, 1½ teaspoons of soy sauce, and 1 tablespoon of sherry in a small bowl. Keep aside.
4. Put the remaining 1 tablespoon of olive oil in the wok and sauté the ginger for about 30 seconds.
5. Add the beef in an even layer and cook for about 2 minutes, until browned.
6. Add the onions and cook for 1 minute more, then transfer the mixture to a plate.
7. Add the broth and green and red peppers to the wok. Cover with a lid and cook for about 1 minute over high heat.
8. Move the beef and onion mixture back to the wok and stir-fry for 1 minute.
9. Dish out and serve immediately.
Serving Suggestions: Serve over brown rice.
Variation Tip: You can also use coconut aminos instead of soy sauce.
Nutritional Information per Serving:
Calories: 215|Fat: 10g|Sat Fat: 3.1g|Carbohydrates: 11g|Fiber: 2g|Sugar: 6g|Protein: 20g

Beef with Broccoli

Prep Time: 10 Minutes
Cook Time: 15 Minutes
Serves: 4
Ingredients:
• 2 tablespoons olive oil
• 2 garlic cloves, minced
• 1-pound beef sirloin steak, sliced into thin strips
• ¼ cup low-sodium chicken broth
• 2 teaspoons ginger, grated
• 1 tablespoon ground flax seeds
• ½ teaspoon red pepper flakes, crushed
• Salt and black pepper, to taste
• 1 large carrot, peeled and thinly sliced
• 2 cups broccoli florets
• 1 scallion, thinly sliced
Preparation:
1. Heat 1 tablespoon of oil to a non-stick skillet over medium-high heat. Add the garlic and sauté it for almost 1 minute.
2. Add the beef and cook for 4–5 minutes or browned. Using a slotted spoon, transfer the beef into a suitable bowl. Remove the excess liquid from the skillet.
3. Mix the broth, ginger, flax seeds, red pepper flakes, salt, and black pepper in a bowl.
4. In the same skillet, heat the remaining oil over medium heat.
5. Add the carrot, broccoli, and broth mixture and cook for 3–4 minutes or until the desired doneness of the vegetables.
6. Stir in the beef and scallion and cook for 3–4 minutes.
7. Transfer the beef mixture into a suitable bowl and set it aside to cool.
8. Evenly divide the mixture into four containers.
9. Cover the containers and refrigerate for 1–2 days. Reheat in the microwave before serving.
Serving Suggestion: Top with sesame seeds.
Variation Tip: Substitute chicken broth with beef broth.
Nutritional Information per Serving:
Calories 211 | Fat 15g | Sodium 151mg | Carbs 7g | Fiber 2g | Sugar 2g | Protein 36g

Mexican Beef Brisket

Prep Time: 5 minutes
Cook Time: 29 minutes
Servings: 5

Ingredients:
- ½ tablespoon chili powder
- ½ tablespoon sugar-free tomato paste
- ½ onion, thinly sliced
- 1½ pounds grass-fed beef boneless brisket, trimmed and cut into 1½-inch cubes
- ½ tablespoon olive oil
- ½ cup homemade beef broth
- Salt and black pepper, to taste
- ¼ cup roasted tomato salsa
- 3 garlic cloves, peeled and smashed

Preparation:
1. Mix the beef, chili powder, salt, and black pepper in a large bowl.
2. Put the olive oil and onions in the pot of a pressure cooker. Press the Sauté function.
3. Sauté for 3 minutes, then add the garlic and tomato paste.
4. Sauté for about 1 minute, then add the beef, salsa, and broth. Turn off the Sauté function.
5. Fasten the lid and cook for 25 minutes at high pressure.
6. Release the pressure naturally and dish out to serve hot.

Serving Suggestions: Serve garnished with chopped coriander.
Variation Tip: You can also make this recipe using pork or chicken.
Nutritional Information per Serving:
Calories: 259|Fat: 18.6g|Sat Fat: 7.5g|Carbohydrates: 3.2g|Fiber: 0.6g|Sugar: 0.7g|Protein: 18.9g

Boneless Pork Chops in Tomato Sauce

Prep Time: 10 minutes
Cook Time: 28 minutes
Servings: 4

Ingredients:
- 2 teaspoons paprika
- 8 thick pork chops, fat rind removed
- 2 chicken bouillon cubes
- 2 teaspoons dried oregano
- 2 yellow onions, cut into rings
- 56 ounces diced canned tomatoes (with their juices)
- 10 ounces low-fat mozzarella cheese
- 8 garlic cloves, sliced
- Salt and black pepper, to taste

Preparation:
1. Preheat the oven to 400°F and lightly grease a deep baking pan.
2. Season the pork chops with salt and black pepper.
3. Grease a skillet with oil and heat over high heat. Add the pork chops and sear them for about 2 minutes per side.
4. Remove the pork chops from the skillet and transfer them to the baking dish.
5. Add the onion rings and garlic to the skillet and sauté them in some oil for about 2 minutes.
6. Add the tomato, bouillon cubes, and spices to the skillet and mix well.
7. Simmer for 2 minutes, then drizzle the mixture over the pork chops.
8. Top with the mozzarella cheese and bake in the preheated oven for 20 minutes.
9. Dish out the pork chops, serve, and enjoy.

Serving Suggestions: Serve over rice.
Variation Tip: You can also use low-fat parmesan cheese.
Nutritional Information per Serving:
Calories: 572|Fat: 19.8g|Sat Fat: 9.8g|Carbohydrates: 28.6g|Fiber: 6.8g|Sugar: 15.3g|Protein: 69g

Cajun Chicken Breast

Prep Time: 10 Minutes
Cook Time: 50 Minutes
Serves: 4

Ingredients:
- 1-pound skinless, boneless chicken breast,
- 1 tablespoon Cajun seasonings
- 1 tablespoon olive oil
- ¼ cup orange juice

Preparation:
1. Preheat the oven to 360℉.
2. Rub the chicken breast with the Cajun seasonings and brush with the olive oil.
3. Place the chicken breast in a roasting pan.
4. Pour the orange juice over the chicken breast and transfer it to the preheated oven.
5. Cook the chicken breast for 50 minutes.
6. Serve and enjoy!

Serving Suggestion: Serve with your favorite veggies.
Variation Tip: Substitute orange juice with lemon juice.
Nutritional Information per Serving:
Calories 166 | Fat 6.4g | Sodium 95mg | Carbs 1.6g | Fiber 0g | Sugar 1.3g | Protein 24.2g

Mushroom Chicken Stew

Prep Time: 10 Minutes
Cook Time: 1 Hour 15 Minutes
Serves: 4

Ingredients:
- 4 chicken breasts
- 1 (6-ounce) can mushrooms
- ½ medium head cabbage, chopped
- 2 medium onions, chopped
- 2 garlic cloves, minced

- Salt and pepper, to taste
- 12 ounces tomato juice

Preparation:
1. Place the chicken breasts in a pressure cooker, cover with water, and pressure cook for 15 minutes.
2. Remove the chicken and shred it using forks.
3. Put the cabbage, mushrooms, and onions in a large saucepan.
4. Add the garlic, salt, and pepper to taste.
5. Add the tomato juice and shredded chicken.
6. Simmer for about 1 hour.
7. Serve.

Serving Suggestion: Garnish with chopped cilantro.
Variation Tip: Feel free to add more seasonings.
Nutritional Information per Serving:
Calories 284 | Fat 4g | Sodium 184mg | Carbs 18g | Fiber 1g | Sugar 5g | Protein 17g

Marinated Turkey Breasts

Prep Time: 15 minutes (plus 30 minutes for marinating)
Cook Time: 8 minutes
Servings: 4

Ingredients:
- ½ teaspoon dried basil
- ½ teaspoon garlic powder
- ½ teaspoon thyme
- 2 teaspoons olive oil
- Salt and black pepper, to taste
- 8 ounces turkey breast, cut into pieces
- 3 teaspoons balsamic vinegar

Preparation:
1. Mix the thyme, basil, garlic powder, olive oil, balsamic vinegar, and pepper in a bowl.
2. Add the turkey pieces, mix well, and allow to marinate for about half an hour.
3. Fry the turkey for about 8 minutes in a skillet over medium heat.
4. Dish out and enjoy!

Serving Suggestions: Serve over your choice of rice, pasta, or veggies.
Variation Tip: You can also make this recipe with chicken breasts.
Nutritional Information per Serving:
Calories: 81|Fat: 3.3g|Sat Fat: 0.5g|Carbohydrates: 2.8g|Fiber: 0.4g|Sugar: 2.1g|Protein: 9.8g

Cheesy Chicken Casserole

Prep Time: 10 Minutes
Cook Time: 40 Minutes
Serves: 6
Ingredients:
• 4 slices bacon, cooked and crumbled
• 3 cups cauliflower florets
• 5 cups water
• 3 cups chicken, cooked and chopped
• 3 cups broccoli florets
• 2 cups reduced-fat cheddar cheese, grated
• 1 cup fat-free sour cream
• 4 tablespoons olive oil
• 1 teaspoon salt
• ½ teaspoon black pepper
• ½ teaspoon garlic powder
• ½ teaspoon paprika
• Non-stick cooking spray
Preparation:
1. Put 5 cups of water in a large saucepan and bring to a boil.
2. Add the cauliflower and cook for 4 to 5 minutes or until tender. Drain well. Repeat with the broccoli.
3. Preheat the oven to 350ºF. Spray a baking dish with the cooking spray.
4. Mash the cauliflower and broccoli with the olive oil, sour cream, and seasonings in a large bowl.
5. Add ½ of the cheese and mix well.
6. Place the cooked chopped chicken into the prepared baking dish. Spread the vegetable mixture on top, then sprinkle with the remaining cheese.
7. Bake for 20–25 minutes or until heated through and cheese is melted.
Serving Suggestion: Top with chopped cilantro.
Variation Tip: Substitute broccoli with asparagus.
Nutritional Information per Serving:
Calories 393 | Fat 21.1g | Sodium 975mg | Carbs 13.4g | Fiber 3.2g | Sugar 5.4g | Protein 38.7g

Jerk Chicken Breasts

Prep Time: 4 Hours 10 Minutes

Cook Time: 15 Minutes
Serves: 4
Ingredients:
• 2 habanero chili peppers, seeded and halved lengthwise
• ½ sweet onion, cut into chunks
• 1 tablespoon garlic, minced
• 1 tablespoon ground allspice
• 2 teaspoons fresh thyme, chopped
• ¼ cup freshly squeezed lime juice
• ½ teaspoon ground nutmeg
• ¼ teaspoon ground cinnamon
• 1 teaspoon freshly ground black pepper
• 2 tablespoons extra-virgin olive oil
• 4 (5-ounce) boneless, skinless chicken breasts
• 2 cups fresh arugula
• 1 cup cherry tomatoes, halved
Preparation:
1. Add the habanero peppers, onion, garlic, allspice, thyme, lime juice, nutmeg, cinnamon, black pepper, and olive oil to a blender. Pulse well.
2. Place the mixture in a large mixing bowl or 2 medium mixing bowls, submerge the chicken breasts in the mixture, and press to coat them thoroughly.
3. Place the bowl(s) in the refrigerator for at least 4 hours to marinate.
4. Preheat the oven to 400℉.
5. Take the bowl(s) out of the fridge and toss out the marinade.
6. Place the chicken breasts on a baking sheet and roast them in the preheated oven for 15 minutes or until golden brown and faintly charred. Midway through the cooking time, rotate the chicken.
7. Allow the chicken to rest for 5 minutes after removing the baking sheet from the oven.
8. Serve on a big platter.
Serving Suggestion: Serve the chicken with the arugula and cherry tomatoes.
Variation Tip: Replace arugula with the same amount of blanched spinach.
Nutritional Information per Serving:
Calories 367| Fat 17.9g | Sodium 135mg| Carbs 7.8g | Fiber 1.6 g | Sugar 2.6g | Protein 42.6g

Chicken Cacciatore

Prep Time: 10 Minutes
Cook Time: 1 Hour
Serves: 6
Ingredients:
• ¼ cup whole-wheat flour
• 1 (2-pound) chicken, cut into 4 breasts, 2 drumsticks, 2 wings, and 2 thighs
• Salt and black pepper, to taste
• 2 tablespoons olive oil
• 3 slices bacon, chopped

- 4 ounces button mushrooms, halved
- 1 sweet onion, chopped
- 2 teaspoons garlic, minced
- ½ cup red wine
- 1 (15-ounce) can low-sodium stewed tomatoes
- Pinch of red pepper flakes
- 2 teaspoons fresh oregano, chopped

Preparation:

1. Put the flour in a large bowl and dredge all of the chicken pieces in it. Season the coated chicken with salt and pepper.
2. Heat the olive oil in a large skillet over medium-high heat.
3. Place the chicken in the skillet and cook for 20 minutes or until all sides are golden brown. Turn the chicken halfway through the cooking time. Transfer the cooked chicken to a plate.
4. Place the bacon in the same skillet and cook for 5 minutes until it curls. Stir from time to time while cooking. Transfer the bacon to the same plate.
5. Add the mushrooms, onion, and garlic to the same skillet and sauté for 4 minutes until tender.
6. Combine the red wine, tomatoes, pepper flakes, and oregano in the skillet. Stir to mix and bring to a boil.
7. Return the chicken and bacon to the skillet. Reduce the heat and simmer for 30 minutes or until the internal temperature of the chicken registers as 165°F.
8. Pour the mixture into a large bowl. Cool for 10 minutes, then serve.

Serving Suggestion: Garnish with chopped cilantro.

Variation Tip: Omit red pepper flakes for a milder dish.

Nutritional Information per Serving:
Calories 418 | Fat 18.9g | Sodium 356mg | Carbs 11g | Fiber 1.5g | Sugar 4.1g | Protein 49.3g

Chicken Arroz

Prep Time: 10 Minutes
Cook Time: 25 Minutes
Serves: 4

Ingredients:
- 1 onion, diced
- 1 red bell pepper, diced
- 2 cups chicken breast, cooked and cubed
- 1 cup cauliflower, grated
- 1 cup peas, thawed
- 2 tablespoons cilantro, diced
- ½ teaspoon lemon zest
- 14½ ounces low-sodium chicken broth
- ¼ cup black olives, sliced
- ¼ cup sherry
- 1 clove garlic, diced
- 2 teaspoons extra-virgin olive oil
- ¼ teaspoon salt
- ¼ teaspoon cayenne pepper

Preparation:

1. Heat the oil in a large skillet over medium-high heat. Add the bell pepper, onion, and garlic and cook for 1 minute.
2. Add the cauliflower and cook, frequently stirring, until light brown, 4–5 minutes.
3. Stir in the broth, sherry, zest, and seasonings and bring to a boil.
4. Reduce the heat, cover, and simmer for 15 minutes.
5. Stir in the chicken, peas, and olives. Cover and simmer another 3–6 minutes or until heated through.
6. Serve and enjoy!

Serving Suggestion: Garnish with cilantro.

Variation Tip: To get the best from this recipe, use a mix of green and black olives.

Nutritional Information per Serving:
Calories 229 | Fat 5.7g | Sodium 306mg | Carbs 13g | Fiber 3.8g | Sugar 5.4g | Protein 24.4g

Chicken Cordon Bleu

Prep Time: 10 Minutes
Cook Time: 25 Minutes
Serves: 4

Ingredients:
- 4 chicken boneless and skinless breast halves
- 4 slices ham
- 1 cup mozzarella cheese, grated
- ½ cup skim milk
- ½ cup fat-free sour cream
- ½ can condensed cream of chicken soup
- ½ cup cornflakes, crushed
- ½ teaspoon lemon juice
- ¼ teaspoon paprika
- ½ teaspoon pepper
- ½ teaspoon garlic powder
- ¼ teaspoon salt
- Non-stick cooking spray

Preparation:

1. Preheat the oven to 350°F.
2. Spray a 13-inch x 9-inch baking dish with cooking spray.
3. Flatten the chicken halves to ¼-inch thick. Sprinkle each piece with pepper and top with a slice of ham and 3 tablespoons of cheese down the middle. Roll up, tuck the ends under, and secure with a toothpick.
4. Pour the milk into a shallow bowl.

5. In a separate shallow bowl, combine the cornflakes and seasonings.

6. Dip each chicken piece in the milk, roll in the cornflake mixture, then place in the prepared baking dish.

7. Bake in the preheated oven for 25–30 minutes or until the chicken is cooked through.

8. Mix the soup, sour cream, and lemon juice until combined in a small saucepan.

9. Cook over medium heat until hot.

10. Remove the toothpicks from the chicken and place the chicken onto serving plates. Top the chicken with the sauce, and serve.

Serving Suggestion: Serve alongside your favorite veggies.

Variation Tip: For a light version, remove the condensed cream of chicken soup from the ingredients.

Nutritional Information per Serving:
Calories 395 | Fat 16.9g | Sodium 727mg | Carbs 13g | Fiber 0.7g | Sugar 4.3g | Protein 43.8g

Cashew Chicken

Prep Time: 10 Minutes
Cook Time: 10 Minutes
Serves: 4

Ingredients:
• 1-pound skinless, boneless chicken breast, cut into cubes
• ½ onion, sliced
• 2 tablespoons green onion, diced
• ½ teaspoon fresh ginger, peeled and grated
• 1 cup whole blanched cashews, toasted
• 1 clove garlic, minced
• 4 tablespoons oil
• 2 tablespoons dark soy sauce
• 2 tablespoons hoisin sauce
• 2 tablespoons water
• 2 teaspoons corn starch
• 2 teaspoons dry sherry
• 1 teaspoon stevia
• 1 teaspoon sesame seed oil

Preparation:
1. Place the chicken cubes in a large bowl and add the corn starch, sherry, and ginger. Stir until well mixed.

2. Whisk together the soy sauce, hoisin, stevia, and water in a small bowl until smooth.

3. Heat the oil in a wok or a large skillet over high heat.

4. Add the garlic and onion and cook, stirring, until the garlic sizzles, about 30 seconds.

5. Stir in the chicken mixture and cook, frequently stirring, until the chicken is almost done, about 2 minutes.

6. Reduce the heat to medium and stir in the sauce mixture.

7. Continue cooking and stirring until everything is blended.

8. Add the cashews and cook for 30 seconds.

9. Drizzle with sesame oil, and cook another 30 seconds, stirring constantly.

10. Serve immediately.

Serving Suggestion: Garnish with green onions.

Variation Tip: Substitute sesame seed oil with peanut oil.

Nutritional Information per Serving:
Calories 483 | Fat 32g | Sodium 846mg | Carbs 19g | Fiber 2.9g | Sugar 5.4g | Protein 32.5g

Curried Chicken Salad with Apples

Prep Time: 5 minutes
Cook Time: 0 minutes
Servings: 3

Ingredients:
• ¼ cup cashews, chopped
• ½ cup plain non-fat Greek yogurt
• ½ tablespoon tahini
• 2 teaspoons curry powder
• ½ teaspoon ground cinnamon
• ½ pound chicken breast, cooked and diced
• ½ Granny Smith apple, diced
• 1 celery stalk, diced
• 1 green onion, diced

Preparation:
1. Whisk the yogurt thoroughly in a large bowl and add the curry powder, tahini, chicken, celery, apple, green onions, cinnamon, and cashews.

2. Mix well and refrigerate for about 1 hour before serving.

Serving Suggestions: Serve with fresh parsley sprinkled on top.

Variation Tip: You can use cooked turkey instead of chicken.

Nutritional Information per Serving:
Calories: 215|Fat: 8.8g|Sat Fat: 1.3g|Carbohydrates: 14.5g|Fiber: 2.8g|Sugar: 7.7g|Protein: 20.6g

Prosciutto-Wrapped Cream Cheese Chicken Breasts

Prep Time: 10 minutes
Cook Time: 30 minutes
Servings: 2

Ingredients:
- 15 fresh basil leaves
- 3 ounces cream cheese
- 2 chicken breasts
- Salt and black pepper, to taste
- 4 ounces prosciutto, finely sliced

Preparation:
1. Preheat the oven to 380°F and grease a baking sheet.
2. Place the prosciutto slices on a piece of aluminum foil and spread the cream cheese evenly over them.
3. Top with the basil leaves, covering the cream cheese.
4. Wrap the prosciutto, cream cheese, and basil leaves around the chicken breasts and sprinkle a little pepper on top.
5. Place the chicken on the baking sheet and bake in the preheated oven for about 30 minutes.
6. Carve the chicken breasts into slices and serve.

Serving Suggestions: Serve with any low-carb dip you prefer.

Variation Tip: You can also make this recipe with turkey breasts.

Nutritional Information per Serving:
Calories: 498|Fat: 28.4g|Sat Fat: 13.2g|Carbohydrates: 2.1g|Fiber: 0.1g|Sugar: 0.1g|Protein: 55.7g

Lemon Chicken Piccata

Prep Time: 5 minutes
Cook Time: 11 minutes
Servings: 1

Ingredients:
- 1 tablespoon low-sodium chicken stock
- 2 tablespoons capers, drained
- 1 tablespoon dry white wine
- 2 tablespoons lemon juice
- 2 tablespoons Italian parsley, minced
- 1½ tablespoons butter, unsalted
- ⅛ teaspoon white pepper
- Salt and black pepper, to taste
- 1 skinless, boneless chicken breast, chopped
- ½ tablespoon all-purpose flour
- 1 tablespoon olive oil

Preparation:
1. Spread the flour onto a dinner plate and season it with salt and black pepper.
2. Dredge the chicken breast slices in the seasoned flour and set them aside.
3. Put the oil in a large sauté pan and cook the chicken breast slices for about 4 minutes per side over medium-high heat.
4. Remove the chicken from the pan and set it aside.
5. Pour the wine, lemon juice, and chicken stock into the sauté pan.
6. Switch the heat to high and boil the mixture for about 3 minutes.
7. Reduce the heat to medium and add the butter, capers, parsley, and chicken breast slices back to the pan.
8. Dish out and serve warm.

Serving Suggestions: Serve over cooked brown rice.

Variation Tip: You can use almond flour instead of all-purpose flour.

Nutritional Information per Serving:
Calories: 880|Fat: 79.7g|Sat Fat: 42.4g|Carbohydrates: 14.6g|Fiber: 2.7g|Sugar: 7g|Protein: 29.3g

Chicken Chili

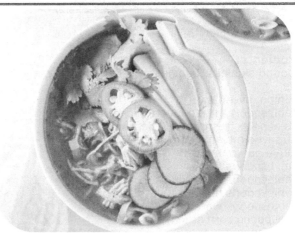

Prep Time: 10 minutes
Cook Time: 15 minutes
Servings: 3

Ingredients:
- ½ teaspoon oregano
- ½ teaspoon ground cumin
- ½ pound skinless, boneless chicken breast
- ½ tablespoon olive oil
- 2 cloves garlic, minced
- 1 avocado, diced
- 4 sprigs cilantro
- 8 ounces salsa verde
- ½ yellow onion, diced
- 1 cup sour cream
- 4 radishes, finely chopped

Preparation:

1. Add the olive oil to an Instant Pot and press select the Sauté function.
2. Add the onions and cook for about 3 minutes, occasionally stirring.
3. Add the garlic, cumin, and oregano and sauté for 2 minutes.
4. Drizzle half of the salsa verde into the pot and top with the chicken breasts.
5. Pour the remaining salsa verde over the chicken.
6. Fasten the lid and select "Pressure Cook."
7. Cook for about 10 minutes, then naturally release the pressure for 5 minutes.
8. Dish out the chicken from the pot and shred with a fork.
9. Put the shredded chicken back into the pot and stir well before serving.
Serving Suggestions: Serve in a bowl topped with the avocado, radish, sour cream, and cilantro.
Variation Tip: You can add veggies of your choice for the topping.
Nutritional Information per Serving:
Calories: 1386|Fat: 79g|Sat Fat: 23.9g|Carbohydrates: 112.5g|Fiber: 11.5g|Sugar: 7.2g|Protein: 65.2g

Chicken and Green Bean Curry

Prep Time: 15 minutes
Cook Time: 23 minutes
Servings: 4
Ingredients:
• 2 garlic cloves, crushed
• 1 tablespoon olive oil
• 2 tablespoons green curry paste
• ½ tablespoon fish sauce
• 2 pounds grass-fed boneless, skinless chicken thighs, cut into 2-inch long, thin slices
• ½ cup coconut cream
• ½ tablespoon soy sauce
• ½ tablespoon fresh lime juice
• 4 ounces unsweetened coconut milk
• 6 ounces green beans, trimmed and cut into 2-inch pieces
• 1 small yellow onion, thinly sliced
• ½ cup homemade chicken broth
• ¼ cup fresh cilantro, chopped
• Salt, to taste
Preparation:

1. Rub the chicken thighs with salt and keep them aside.
2. Put the olive oil in a non-stick skillet and sauté the garlic over medium-high heat for 30 seconds.
3. Add the onions and sauté for 3 minutes.
4. Add the curry paste and coconut cream and cook for about 4 minutes, occasionally stirring.
5. Add the coconut milk, chicken, broth, and both sauces.
6. Secure the lid and cook for about 12 minutes on medium-low heat.
7. Add the lime juice and green beans and cook for about 3 minutes.
8. Remove from the heat, then top with cilantro and avocado slices.
9. Dish out and serve hot.
Serving Suggestions: Serve over brown rice.
Variation Tip: You can use turkey instead of chicken.
Nutritional Information per Serving:
Calories: 290|Fat: 16.4g|Sat Fat: 6.6g|Carbohydrates: 6.6g|Fiber: 1.7g|Sugar: 1.8g|Protein: 31.5g

Spicy Whole Chicken

Prep Time: 30 minutes
Cook Time: 40 minutes
Servings: 4
Ingredients:
• 1 teaspoon red pepper flakes, crushed
• 1 teaspoon ground cumin
• ½ tablespoon fresh rosemary, minced
• Salt and black pepper, to taste
• 1-pound grass-fed whole chicken, neck and giblets removed
• 1 teaspoon cayenne pepper
• 1 tablespoon olive oil
Preparation:
1. Preheat the oven to 325°F.
2. Mix the ground cumin, rosemary, red pepper flakes, cayenne pepper, salt, and black pepper in a bowl.
3. Rub the chicken generously with the spice mixture and drizzle with olive oil.
4. Wrap aluminum foil around the chicken and place it on a baking sheet.
5. Bake for about 40 minutes in the preheated oven.

6. Place the cooked chicken onto a cutting board, then slice it into desired-sized slices.

7. Serve and enjoy!

Serving Suggestions: Serve over brown rice.

Variation Tip: You can increase the amount of spice and seasonings according to your taste.

Nutritional Information per Serving:
Calories: 249|Fat: 18g|Sat Fat: 5.6g|Carbohydrates: 1g|Fiber: 0.5g|Sugar: 0.1g|Protein: 21.5g

Turkey Meatballs

Prep Time: 10 minutes
Cook Time: 25 minutes
Servings: 4

Ingredients:
- 4 tablespoons fresh parsley, chopped
- ½ teaspoon mustard powder
- ¼ red onion, chopped
- ¼ teaspoon cumin
- ½ teaspoon thyme
- ¼ teaspoon turmeric
- 10 ounces ground turkey
- 2 tablespoons oats
- 1 celery stick, chopped
- 1½ cloves garlic, chopped
- ¼ teaspoon chipotle pepper, chopped
- 1½ ounces fresh spinach, chopped
- 1 egg whites
- ¼ green bell pepper, chopped
- Salt and black pepper, to taste

Preparation:
1. Preheat the oven to 350°F and grease a baking sheet with olive oil.
2. Put the onion, garlic, spinach, peppers, and celery in a large bowl. Mix well.
3. Add the turkey, egg whites, oats, and spices to the bowl and mix well.
4. Shape the turkey mixture into balls and arrange them in a single layer on the baking sheet.
5. Bake for 25 minutes in the preheated oven.

Serving Suggestions: Serve topped with fresh coriander.

Variation Tip: You can also use frozen spinach.

Nutritional Information per Serving:
Calories: 179|Fat: 8.4g|Sat Fat: 1.4g|Carbohydrates: 6.7g|Fiber: 1.9g|Sugar: 1.2g|Protein: 22.5g

Stuffed Chicken Breasts

Prep Time: 10 minutes
Cook Time: 20 minutes
Servings: 2

Ingredients:
- 2 canned artichoke hearts
- ½ teaspoon curry powder
- 2 chicken breasts, slit cut across each about ¾ of the way through
- 10 large basil leaves, chopped
- 2 ounces mozzarella cheese, chopped
- 2 garlic cloves, chopped
- Salt and black pepper, to taste
- 2 teaspoons sundried tomatoes, chopped
- ½ teaspoon paprika

Preparation:
1. Preheat the oven to 365°F and grease a baking sheet with olive oil.
2. Meanwhile, mix the mozzarella cheese, artichoke, tomato, basil, and garlic and combine well.
3. Stuff the mixture in the slits made in the chicken breasts, then secure the breasts with toothpicks.
4. Put the stuffed chicken breasts on the baking sheet and season with the pepper, paprika, and curry powder.
5. Bake for about 20 minutes in the preheated oven or until cooked through.
6. Discard the toothpicks and serve the chicken warm.

Serving Suggestions: Serve with steamed broccoli.

Variation Tip: You can use regular tomatoes if you can't get sundried ones.

Nutritional Information per Serving:
Calories: 440|Fat: 16g|Sat Fat: 6g|Carbohydrates: 21.1g|Fiber: 9.8g|Sugar: 2.2g|Protein: 55.3g

Turkey Stir-Fry

Prep Time: 10 Minutes
Cook Time: 25 Minutes
Serves: 5

Ingredients:
• 12 ounces turkey fillet, sliced
• 1 carrot, julienned
• 1 onion, sliced
• 1 teaspoon potato starch
• ½ cup low-sodium chicken broth
• 1 teaspoon chili powder
• 1 tablespoon avocado oil

Preparation:
1. Put the avocado oil in a saucepan over medium heat and add the sliced turkey.
2. Cook the turkey for 2 minutes, stirring occasionally, then add the carrot, onion, and chili powder.
3. Stir the ingredients well and cook them for 10 minutes.
4. Meanwhile, whisk the chicken broth and potato starch.
5. Pour the liquid over the turkey mixture and stir well.
6. Cook the mixture for 10 minutes more.
7. Serve hot.

Serving Suggestion: Garnish with chopped green onions.
Variation Tip: Substitute turkey fillet with chicken breast.
Nutritional Information per Serving:
Calories 89 | Fat 0.8g | Sodium 176mg | Carbs 4.8g | Fiber 1.1g | Sugar 1.6g | Protein 14.8g

Ground Turkey Stir-Fry

Prep Time: 10 Minutes
Cook Time: 20 Minutes
Serves: 4
Ingredients:

• 1 teaspoon olive oil
• 1-pound 93% lean ground turkey
• 1 courgette, halved and cut into slices
• 1 large red bell pepper, sliced
• 1 large green bell pepper, sliced
• ½ onion, finely chopped
• 2 teaspoons garlic, crushed
• 2 teaspoons oregano, fresh or dried
• 1 cup lentils, cooked
• ¼ cup black olives, pitted and halved
• 1 tablespoon balsamic vinegar
• 1 cup spinach, roughly chopped
• Sea salt and black pepper, to taste

Preparation:
1. Heat the olive oil in a large, heavy-bottom pan on medium-high heat until hot.
2. Add the ground turkey, courgette, red and green bell peppers, onion, garlic, and oregano, and cook for 10 minutes until the turkey is cooked through and the vegetables are tender.
3. Add the cooked lentils, pitted olives, and balsamic vinegar and cook for 5 minutes until heated through.
4. Remove from the heat, stir in the chopped spinach, and let it sit for 5 minutes until the greens are wilted.
5. Season with ground sea salt and ground black pepper and serve.

Serving Suggestion: Garnish with basil leaves.
Variation Tip: You can use capers in place of olives.
Nutritional Information per Serving:
Calories 389 | Fat 11.1g | Sodium 235mg | Carbs 37.7g | Fiber 17.4g | Sugar 5g | Protein 36.5g

Turkey Tacos

Prep Time: 10 Minutes
Cook Time: 20 Minutes
Serves: 4
Ingredients:
• 3 tablespoons extra-virgin olive oil
• 1-pound ground turkey
• 1 onion, chopped
• 1 green bell pepper, seeded and chopped
• ½ teaspoon sea salt
• 1 small head cauliflower, grated
• 1 cup corn kernels
• ½ cup prepared salsa
• 1 cup shredded pepper Jack cheese

Preparation:
1. Heat the olive oil in a large non-stick skillet over medium-high heat until shiny. Add the turkey.
2. Cook the turkey, occasionally stirring with a wooden spoon, until browned, about 5 minutes.

3. Add the onion, pepper, and salt. Cook, occasionally stirring, for 4–5 minutes, until the vegetables are tender.

4. Add the cauliflower, corn, and salsa. Cook, constantly stirring, until the cauliflower rice is tender, about 3 minutes more. Sprinkle with cheese.

5. Reduce the heat to low, cover, and let the cheese melt for 2–3 minutes.

Serving Suggestion: Garnish with chopped cilantro.

Variation Tip: Substitute ground turkey with ground chicken.

Nutritional Information per Serving:
Calories 517 | Fat 34g | Sodium 773mg | Carbs 17.6g | Fiber 4.2g | Sugar 6.5g | Protein 42.7g

Turkey Posole

Prep Time: 10 minutes
Cook Time: 26 minutes
Servings: 4

Ingredients:
- ¾ cup red or green sweet pepper, chopped
- ½ cup fresh poblano chili pepper, chopped
- 1-pound turkey breast, ground
- ½ cup onion, chopped
- 2 teaspoons olive oil
- 1 teaspoon dried oregano, crushed
- ½ teaspoon cumin, ground
- ¼ teaspoon cinnamon, ground
- 1 (15½-ounce) can golden hominy, rinsed and drained
- 1 (8-ounce) can no-salt-added tomato sauce
- ¼ cup radish, thinly sliced
- 2 teaspoons unsweetened cocoa powder
- ½ teaspoon salt
- ½ teaspoon ancho chili pepper, ground
- 2 (14½-ounce) cans no-salt-added diced tomatoes, undrained
- 1 cup reduced-sodium chicken broth
- ¼ cup green onions, sliced
- Lime wedges, for serving

Preparation:
1. Heat the olive oil in a Dutch oven over medium heat and cook the turkey, sweet pepper, onion, and poblano chili for about 5 minutes.

2. Add the cocoa powder, salt, oregano, cumin, ancho chili pepper, and cinnamon, and cook for about 1 minute.

3. Add the tomatoes, hominy, water, and tomato sauce, and let it reach a boil.

4. Reduce the heat, secure the lid and simmer for about 20 minutes, occasionally stirring.

5. Serve garnished with green onions, radishes, and lime wedges.

Serving Suggestions: Serve hot with bread, couscous, or rice.

Variation Tip: You can use any other spice if you don't like poblano.

Nutritional Information per Serving:
Calories: 271|Fat: 4.2g|Sat Fat: 0.9g|Carbohydrates: 30g|Fiber: 9.1g|Sugar: 12.4g|Protein: 31.1g

Turkey Tostadas

Prep Time: 10 minutes
Cook Time: 15 minutes
Servings: 4

Ingredients:
- 2 cups ground turkey, browned and drained
- 2 cups cooked turkey, cut into bite-sized pieces
- 2 tablespoons taco seasoning
- 4 corn tortillas
- ¼ cup low-fat Monterey Jack cheese, shredded
- ½ cup lettuce, shredded
- ½ cup taco sauce
- 1½ cups water
- ¼ cup low-fat refried beans
- ½ cup tomatoes, chopped
- 2 tablespoons onion, chopped

Preparation:
1. Preheat the oven to 380°F and grease a baking sheet.

2. In a large skillet, cook the turkey, taco seasoning, and water over medium heat.

3. Let the mixture reach a boil, reduce the heat, and simmer for 5 minutes, occasionally stirring.

4. Place the tortillas on the prepared baking sheet and bake in the preheated oven for about 7 minutes.

5. Layer the beans over the baked tortillas and top with a quarter of the meat mixture, then the cheese.

6. Put the tortillas back into the oven and bake for about 3 minutes.

7. Take out and top with the tomatoes, lettuce, onions, and taco sauce before serving.

Serving Suggestions: Serve garnished with yogurt and guacamole.

Variation Tip: You can also use low-fat cheddar cheese.

Nutritional Information per Serving:
Calories: 230|Fat: 4g|Sat Fat: 4g|Carbohydrates: 20g|Fiber: 3g|Sugar: 3.8g|Protein: 26g

Poached Salmon

Prep Time: 10 Minutes
Cook Time: 12 Minutes
Serves: 6
Ingredients:
• 1-pound salmon fillet, chopped
• 1 cup organic almond milk
• ¼ cup fresh cilantro, chopped
• ¼ teaspoon cumin seeds
Preparation:
1. Bring the milk to boil and add the cumin seeds and cilantro.
2. When the mixture starts to boil, add the chopped salmon fillet and poach it for 9 minutes over medium heat.
Serving Suggestion: Garnish with more chopped cilantro and some lime slices.
Variation Tip: Substitute almond milk with soy milk.
Nutritional Information per Serving:
Calories 210 | Fat 9.8g | Sodium 187mg | Carbs 1.4g | Fiber 0.9g | Sugar 1.4g | Protein 29.5g

Blackened Cod

Prep Time: 10 Minutes
Cook Time: 20 Minutes
Serves: 4
Ingredients:
• 1-pound cod fillet
• 2 tablespoons olive oil
• ½ teaspoon chili flakes
• ½ teaspoon ground nutmeg
• ½ teaspoon ground cumin
Preparation:
1. Preheat the oven to 365℉.

2. Mix the chili flakes, ground nutmeg, and ground cumin in a small bowl.
3. Rub the cod with the spice mixture and sprinkle with olive oil.
4. Put the coated fish on a baking tray and bake in the preheated oven for 20 minutes.
5. Slice the cod and serve.
Serving Suggestion: Top with chopped cilantro.
Variation Tip: Omit chili flakes for a milder dish.
Nutritional Information per Serving:
Calories 154 | Fat 8.2g | Sodium 71mg | Carbs 0.3g | Fiber 0.1g | Sugar 0.1g | Protein 20.3g

Fish Stew

Prep Time: 10 Minutes
Cook Time: 20 Minutes
Serves: 4
Ingredients:
• 1 tablespoon olive oil
• 1 red bell pepper, seeded and chopped
• 1 onion, chopped
• 3 celery stalks, chopped
• 1 tablespoon garlic, minced
• 2 teaspoons ground cumin
• 6 cups low-sodium vegetable broth
• 1 (15-ounce) can no-salt-added diced tomatoes
• 1 (15-ounce) can low-sodium lentils, drained and rinsed
• 12 ounces salmon, cubed
• Freshly ground black pepper, to taste
Preparation:
1. In a large stockpot, heat the oil over medium-high heat.
2. Add the bell pepper, onion, celery, garlic, and cumin. Sauté for about 4 minutes until softened.
3. Stir in the broth, tomatoes and their juices, and lentils and bring to a boil.
4. Reduce the heat to medium-low and simmer for 10 minutes.
5. Add the fish and simmer for about 6 minutes, until just cooked through.
6. Season with pepper and serve.
Serving Suggestion: Top with fresh cilantro or other fresh herbs of your choice.
Variation Tip: Try any firm fish for this stew, such as halibut, haddock, or trout, as well as shrimp or scallops.
Nutritional Information per Serving:
Calories 396 | Fat 16g | Sodium 357mg | Carbs 40g | Fiber 12g | Sugar 16g | Protein 24g

Grilled Tuna Steaks

Prep Time: 10 Minutes
Cook Time: 8 Minutes
Serves: 6
Ingredients:
• 6 ounces tuna steaks
• 3 tablespoons fresh basil, diced
• 4½ teaspoons olive oil
• ¾ teaspoon salt
• ¼ teaspoon pepper
• Non-stick cooking spray
Preparation:
1. Preheat the broiler on medium. Using cooking spray, coat a baking sheet.
2. Drizzle the oil on all sides of the tuna. Add the basil and season to taste with salt and pepper. Place the fish on the baking sheet.
3. Broil for 5 minutes per side on the third rack of the oven; the tuna should be slightly pink in the center.
4. Serve and enjoy!
Serving Suggestion: Serve with lemon slices.
Variation Tip: Replace tuna with halibut or trout.
Nutritional Information per Serving:
Calories 84 | Fat 5.4g | Sodium 305mg | Carbs 0.1g | Fiber 0 g | Sugar 0g | Protein 8.5g

Crab Cakes

Prep Time: 10 Minutes
Cook Time: 10 Minutes
Serves: 8
Ingredients:
• 1-pound lump blue crab meat
• 1 tablespoon red bell pepper, finely diced
• 1 tablespoon green bell pepper, finely diced
• 1 tablespoon fresh parsley, finely chopped
• 2 eggs
• ¼ teaspoon fresh lemon juice
• ¼ cup Dijon mustard

• 1 tablespoon mayonnaise
• 2 tablespoons sunflower oil
• 1 tablespoon baking powder
• 1 tablespoon Worcestershire sauce
• 1½ teaspoons Old Bay Seasoning
Preparation:
1. In a small bowl, whisk together the Dijon mustard, Worcestershire sauce, and lemon juice until combined. Cover and chill until ready to serve.
2. In a large bowl, mix the crab meat, bell peppers, parsley, eggs, mayonnaise, baking powder, and Old Bay Seasoning until well combined.
3. Heat the oil in a large skillet over medium-high heat.
4. Once the oil is hot, drop 2 tablespoons of the crab mixture into the skillet. The mixture will be loose at first but will hold together as the egg cooks.
5. Cook for 2 minutes or until firm, then flip and cook for another minute.
6. Transfer to a serving plate. Repeat with the rest of the crab mixture.
Serving Suggestion: Serve with mustard dipping sauce.
Variation Tip: Replace Dijon mustard with light mayonnaise.
Nutritional Information per Serving:
Calories 110 | Fat 5.1g | Sodium 468mg | Carbs 3.5g | Fiber 0.7g | Sugar 1.7g | Protein 12.1g

Cajun Baked Catfish

Prep Time: 10 Minutes
Cook Time: 30 Minutes
Serves: 2
Ingredients:
• 2 tablespoons cornmeal
• 2 teaspoons Cajun seasoning
• ¼ teaspoon lemon pepper seasoning
• 2 catfish fillets
• ½ teaspoon dried thyme
• ½ teaspoon dried basil
• ¼ teaspoon garlic powder
• ¼ teaspoon paprika
Preparation:
1. Preheat the oven to 400℉. Coat a non-stick baking tray with cooking spray
2. In a small mixing dish, mix the first 6 ingredients. Coat the fillets on both sides with the mixture.
3. Place the coated fish on the prepared baking tray.
4. Bake the salmon in the preheated oven for 25 minutes or until it flakes easily with a fork.
Serving Suggestion: Serve with your favorite greens.
Variation Tip: Substitute catfish fillets with tilapia fillets.
Nutritional Information per Serving:
Calories 204 | Fat 2.3g | Sodium 473mg | Carbs 8.3g | Fiber 0.8g | Sugar 0.2g | Protein 37.9g

Baked Sea Bass

Prep Time: 1 Hour 10 Minutes
Cook Time: 20 Minutes
Serves: 4
Ingredients:
- 1 (1¼-pound) whole sea bass, gutted
- Salt and black pepper, to taste
- 3 bay leaves
- 1 thyme sprig
- 1 parsley sprig
- 1 rosemary sprig
- 1 tablespoon olive oil
- 1 tablespoon lemon juice
Preparation:
1. Evenly season the cavity and outer side of the fish with salt and black pepper.
2. Cover the fish using plastic wrap and refrigerate for almost 1 hour.
3. Preheat the oven to 450℉.
4. Lightly grease a baking dish. Arrange 2 bay leaves in the bottom of the prepared baking dish.
5. Put the herb sprigs and the remaining bay leaf inside the cavity of the fish.
6. Arrange the fish over the bay leaves in the baking dish and drizzle with the oil.
7. Roast for 15–20 minutes in the preheated oven or until the fish is cooked through.
8. Remove the baking dish from the oven and place the fish onto a platter.
Serving Suggestion: Serve the fish with a drizzle of lemon juice and some greens.
Variation Tip: Substitute sea bass with red snapper.
Nutritional Information per Serving:
Calories 341 | Fat 10.7g | Sodium 208mg | Carbs 1.7g | Fiber 0.9g | Sugar 0.1g | Protein 58g

Citrus-Glazed Trout

Prep Time: 10 Minutes
Cook Time: 25 Minutes
Serves: 4

Ingredients:
- 1 (1½-pound) wild-caught trout, gutted and cleaned
- Salt and black pepper, to taste
- ½ lemon, sliced
- 1 tablespoon fresh dill, minced
- 1 tablespoon olive oil
- ½ tablespoon lemon juice
Preparation:
1. Preheat the oven to 475℉.
2. Place a suitable wire rack onto a foil-lined baking sheet.
3. Generously rub the trout with salt and black pepper, inside and out.
4. Fill the cavity of each fish with the lemon slices and dill.
5. Place the trout onto the prepared baking sheet and drizzle with the oil and lemon juice.
6. Bake in the preheated oven for around 25 minutes.
7. Remove the baking sheet from the oven and transfer the trout onto a serving platter.
8. Serve hot.
Serving Suggestion: Serve with green beans.
Variation Tip: Feel free to add more seasoning.
Nutritional Information per Serving:
Calories 237 | Fat 9.5g | Sodium 55mg | Carbs 1.2g | Fiber 0.3g | Sugar 0.2g | Protein 35.1g

Glazed Scallops

Prep Time: 10 Minutes
Cook Time: 7 Minutes
Serves: 1
Ingredients:
- ¼ pound sea scallops, side muscles removed
- Salt and black pepper, to taste
- ½ tablespoon olive oil
- 1 garlic clove, minced
Preparation:
1. Sprinkle the scallops evenly with salt and black pepper.
2. Heat ½ tablespoon of the oil in a suitable sauté pan over medium-high heat, then sauté the garlic for around 1 minute.
3. Add the scallops and cook for 2–3 minutes per side.
4. Serve hot.
Serving Suggestion: Garnish with fresh cilantro or parsley.
Variation Tip: Feel free to add chili for a hotter flavor.
Nutritional Information per Serving:
Calories 165 | Fat 7.9g | Sodium 183mg | Carbs 3.7g | Fiber 0.1g | Sugar 0g | Protein 19.2g

Herbed Halibut

Prep Time: 10 Minutes
Cook Time: 8 Minutes
Serves: 3

Ingredients:
- ¼ teaspoon dried oregano, crushed
- ¼ teaspoon dried basil, crushed
- ¼ teaspoon dried rosemary, crushed
- Salt and black pepper, to taste
- ½ tablespoon olive oil
- ½ tablespoon lemon juice
- 1 (4-ounce) halibut fillet

Preparation:
1. Add all the recipe ingredients except the halibut fillet to a bowl and mix well.
2. Add the halibut fillet and generously coat it with the marinade.
3. Put the halibut in a bowl, cover it, and refrigerate to marinate for at least 1 hour.
4. Preheat a greased grill pan over medium-high heat.
5. Place the halibut fillet onto the grill pan and cook for almost 4 minutes per side.
6. Serve hot.

Serving Suggestion: Serve with lemon wedges.
Variation Tip: Substitute halibut with trout.
Nutritional Information per Serving:
Calories 275 | Fat 7.7g | Sodium 121mg | Carbs 0.2g | Fiber 0.1g | Sugar 0.1g | Protein 48g

Baked Mackerel

Prep Time: 10 Minutes
Cook Time: 20 Minutes
Serves: 2

Ingredients:
- 1 (6-ounce) mackerel fillet
- ½ tablespoon olive oil
- Salt and black pepper, to taste

Preparation:
1. Preheat the oven to 350℉.
2. Arrange the rack in the middle portion of the oven and lightly grease a baking dish.
3. Brush the fish fillet with the oil and then season with salt and black pepper.
4. Put the fish into the prepared baking dish.
5. Bake in the preheated oven for 16–20 minutes.
6. Serve hot.

Serving Suggestion: Serve with roast potatoes
Variation Tip: Feel free to add more seasoning.
Nutritional Information per Serving:
Calories 253 | Fat 18.7g | Sodium 71mg | Carbs 0g | Fiber 0g | Sugar 0g | Protein 20.3g

Shrimp in Coconut Curry

Prep Time: 20 Minutes
Cook Time: 25 Minutes
Serves: 4

Ingredients:
- 1-pound extra-large shrimp, peeled and deveined
- 1 onion, finely diced
- 1¾ cups unsweetened coconut milk,
- 2 tablespoons fresh lemon juice
- 1 tablespoon fresh ginger, grated
- 1 (14½-ounce) can tomatoes, diced
- 3 cloves garlic, minced
- 1 tablespoon olive oil
- 2 teaspoons ground coriander
- 1 teaspoon curry powder
- Salt, to taste
- ½ teaspoons turmeric
- ¾ teaspoon black pepper
- ¼ teaspoon cayenne

Preparation:
1. In a medium bowl, combine the lemon juice, ¼ teaspoon of salt, ¼ teaspoon of pepper, and cayenne pepper.
2. Add the shrimp and toss to coat, then cover and refrigerate for at least 10 minutes.
3. Heat the oil in a large, deep skillet over medium-high heat. Add the onion and cook until it softens, about 2–3 minutes.
4. Add the remaining seasonings and cook for 1 minute more.
5. Add the tomatoes with their juices and the coconut milk, then stir and bring to a boil. Cook, occasionally stirring, for 5 minutes.
6. Add the shrimp and marinade and cook until the shrimp turn pink, about 2–3 minutes.
7. Serve.

Serving Suggestion: Serve with cauliflower rice.
Variation Tip: Omit cayenne for a milder dish.
Nutritional Information per Serving:
Calories 397 | Fat 28.7g | Sodium 839mg | Carbs 15.6g | Fiber 4.2g | Sugar 10.5g | Protein 24.1g

Zesty Salmon

Prep Time: 10 Minutes
Cook Time: 10 Minutes
Serves: 1

Ingredients:
• ½ tablespoon olive oil
• ⅓ tablespoon lime juice
• ¼ teaspoon Worcestershire sauce
• ¼ teaspoon lime zest, grated finely
• 1 (6-ounce) salmon fillet
• Salt and black pepper, to taste

Preparation:
1. Place the oil, lemon juice, Worcestershire sauce, and lemon zest in a small baking dish and mix well.
2. Coat the fillet with the mixture, then arrange it skin side-up in the baking dish. Set aside for almost 15 minutes.
3. Preheat the broiler of the oven. Arrange the oven rack about 6 inches below the heating element.
4. Line a broiler pan with a piece of foil.
5. Remove the salmon fillet from the baking dish and season with salt and black pepper.
6. Arrange the salmon fillet onto the prepared broiler pan, skin side down. Broil for 8–10 minutes.
7. Serve hot.

Serving Suggestion: Serve with a salad.
Variation Tip: Substitute Worcestershire sauce with balsamic vinegar.
Nutritional Information per Serving:
Calories 290 | Fat 17.5g | Sodium 89mg | Carbs 1.6g | Fiber 0.2g | Sugar 0.5g | Protein 33.1g

Baked Haddock

Prep Time: 10 Minutes
Cook Time: 8 Minutes
Serves: 1

Ingredients:
• 1 (6-ounce) haddock fillet
• Salt and black pepper, to taste
• ½ tablespoon olive oil

Preparation:
1. Evenly season the haddock fillet with salt and black pepper.
2. In a small non-stick skillet, heat the olive oil over medium-high heat. Cook the haddock fillet for 3–4 minutes per side or until the desired doneness.
3. Serve hot.

Serving Suggestion: Serve with green peas
Variation Tip: Substitute haddock with flounder or sole.
Nutritional Information per Serving:
Calories 251 | Fat 8.5g | Sodium 148mg | Carbs 0.1g | Fiber 0g | Sugar 0g | Protein 41.2g

Tuna Niçoise Salad

Prep Time: 5 minutes
Cook Time: 5 minutes
Servings: 2

Ingredients:
• ½ cup black olives, pitted and sliced
• ½ radish, cut into dice-sized pieces
• 2 tablespoons parsley, chopped
• ½ teaspoon balsamic vinegar
• ¼ teaspoon pepper
• 1 whole egg, boiled, cut into dice-sized pieces
• 1-ounce green beans, ends trimmed
• ¼ red bell pepper, sliced
• ½ teaspoon olive oil
• ¼ teaspoon Dijon mustard
• 2 ounces tuna steak, sliced
• 1½ ounces baby spinach
• 1-ounce broccoli, cut into florets
• 1½ ounces cucumber, cut into dice-sized pieces

Preparation:
1. Steam the broccoli and green beans and keep them aside to cool.
2. Season the tuna with pepper on all sides and cook for 2 minutes per side with a little oil in a pan on high heat.
3. Put the beans, broccoli, olives, spinach, cucumber, bell pepper, radish, and egg in a large salad bowl.
4. Add the tuna to the salad along with the olive oil, balsamic vinegar, mustard, salt, and black pepper. Mix well.
5. Serve garnished with the parsley.

Serving Suggestions: Serve the vinaigrette over the salad, or you can use it as a dipping sauce.
Variation Tip: You can also add chopped walnuts.
Nutritional Information per Serving:
Calories: 145|Fat: 6.2g|Sat Fat: 1.5g|Carbohydrates: 9.7g|Fiber: 3.5g|Sugar: 3.1g|Protein: 15g

Citrus Glazed Salmon

Prep Time: 10 minutes plus 1 hour for marinating
Cook Time: 15 minutes
Servings: 2

Ingredients:
- ½ cup white wine
- ½ teaspoon fresh ginger, minced
- ½ tablespoon olive oil
- 2 (2-ounce each) salmon fillets
- 1 tablespoon fresh orange juice
- Black pepper, to taste
- 1 teaspoon fresh orange zest, finely grated

Preparation:
1. Mix all the ingredients in a large bowl except the salmon fillets.
2. Add the salmon and let it marinate in the mixture for about 1 hour.
3. Move the marinated salmon fillets to a non-stick pan coated with oil and cook for about 15 minutes on both sides, occasionally turning.
4. Top the salmon fillets with the marinade before serving.

Serving Suggestions: Garnish with dill, parsley, and lemon wedges.
Variation Tip: You can also use cod in this recipe.
Nutritional Information per Serving:
Calories: 160|Fat: 7.1g|Sat Fat: 1g|Carbohydrates: 3g|Fiber: 0.2g|Sugar: 1.1g|Protein: 11.2g

Shrimp Curry

Prep Time: 10 minutes
Cook Time: 12 minutes
Servings: 6

Ingredients:
- 1 teaspoon ground turmeric
- 1 medium onion, chopped
- Pinch of salt

- 1 tablespoon olive oil
- 1½ teaspoons red chili powder
- 2 pounds shrimp, peeled and deveined
- 1 tablespoon fresh lemon juice
- ¼ cup water
- ½ teaspoon ground cumin
- 2 medium tomatoes, chopped
- ¼ cup fresh cilantro, chopped

Preparation:
1. Put the olive oil on medium-high heat in an Instant Pot and cook the onions, bell pepper, carrot, celery, and garlic for about 3 minutes on "Sauté" mode.
2. Add the spices and cook for about 1 minute.
3. Add the tomatoes and cook for about 2 minutes.
4. Add the water and cook for about 3 minutes.
5. Stir in the shrimp and secure the lid.
6. Cook on high pressure for 3 minutes.
7. Naturally release the pressure and add the cilantro and lemon juice.
8. Dish out and serve hot.

Serving Suggestions: Serve with steamed rice.
Variation Tip: You can use any variety of shrimp.
Nutritional Information per Serving:
Calories: 189|Fat: 4.7g|Sat Fat: 0.4g|Carbohydrates: 5g|Fiber: 1.8g|Sugar: 2.1g|Protein: 33.3g

Sweet and Sour Fish

Prep Time: 10 minutes
Cook Time: 14 minutes
Servings: 3

Ingredients:
- ¼ cup butter
- 2 drops liquid stevia
- 1-pound fish chunks
- Salt and black pepper, to taste
- 1 tablespoon vinegar

Preparation:
1. Put the butter in a large non-stick skillet and cook the fish chunks for about 3 minutes over medium-high heat.
2. Add the stevia and vinegar and cook for about 1 minute.
3. Season with salt and black pepper and cook for about 10 minutes, stirring the fish continuously.
4. Serve immediately and enjoy.

Serving Suggestions: Serve over fried rice.
Variation Tip: You can use any variety of fish you prefer.
Nutritional Information per Serving:
Calories: 274|Fat: 15.4g|Sat Fat: 9.7g|Carbohydrates: 2.8g|Fiber: 0g|Sugar: 0g|Protein: 33.2g

Baked Paprika Shrimp

Prep Time: 5 minutes (plus 30 minutes for marinating)
Cook Time: 15 minutes
Servings: 6
Ingredients:
• 1 teaspoon smoked paprika
• 6 tablespoons butter, melted
• 2 pounds tiger shrimp
• Salt, to taste
Preparation:
1. Preheat the oven to 400°F and lightly grease a baking dish with butter.
2. Mix all the ingredients in a large bowl except for the shrimp. Add the shrimp and allow it to marinate for about 30 minutes.
3. Put the marinated shrimp in the baking dish cook in the preheated oven for about 15 minutes.
4. Serve and enjoy!
Serving Suggestions: Serve warm with your choice of low-fat dip.
Variation Tip: You can adjust the spices according to your taste.
Nutritional Information per Serving:
Calories: 173|Fat: 8.3g|Sat Fat: 1.3g|Carbohydrates: 0.1g|Fiber: 0.1g|Sugar: 0g|Protein: 23.8g

Ginger-Garlic Fish

Prep Time: 10 minutes
Cook Time: 30 minutes
Servings: 3
Ingredients:
• 2 tablespoons ginger-garlic paste
• 3 green chilies, chopped
• 1-pound salmon fillets
• Salt and black pepper, to taste
• Olive oil
Preparation:
1. Rub the salmon fillets with the ginger-garlic paste, salt, and black pepper. Drizzle with some olive oil and sprinkle over the green chilies.
2. Preheat the broiler and put the rack in the high position.
3. Heat a little olive oil in a non-stick skillet over medium heat. Add the salmon fillets skin side down and cook for about 3 minutes.
4. Position the salmon fillets under the preheated broiler and cook for around 7 minutes
5. Serve immediately.
Serving Suggestions: Serve garnished with fresh cilantro.
Variation Tip: You can make this recipe with any fish of your choice.
Nutritional Information per Serving:
Calories: 676|Fat: 61.2g|Sat Fat: 30.5g|Carbohydrates: 3.2g|Fiber: 0.2g|Sugar: 0.2g|Protein: 30.4g

Air-Fried Cod

Prep Time: 5 minutes
Cook Time: 8 minutes
Servings: 3
Ingredients:
• 4 garlic cloves, minced
• 6 eggs, whisked
• 2 small onions, finely chopped
• 3 (4-ounce) skinless cod fillets, cut into rectangular pieces
• 2 green chilies, finely chopped
• 2 teaspoons soy sauce
• ¼ cup low-fat butter
• Salt and black pepper, to taste
Preparation:
1. Set the temperature of an air fryer to 375°F.
2. Mix all the ingredients in a shallow dish except for the cod.
3. Dip each cod fillet in the mixture, then arrange them in a single layer in the air fryer basket.
4. Cook for about 8 minutes.
Serving Suggestions: Serve with a low-fat yogurt dip.
Variation Tip: You can also use salmon with this recipe.
Nutritional Information per Serving:
Calories: 529|Fat: 34.2g|Sat Fat: 12.5g|Carbohydrates: 30.8g|Fiber: 2.2g|Sugar: 5g|Protein: 24.3g

Lemongrass Shrimp Skewers

Prep Time: 10 minutes plus 2 hours for marinating
Cook Time: 15 minutes
Servings: 3

Ingredients:
- 2 tablespoons butter
- ½ teaspoon smoked paprika
- 1-pound shrimp, peeled and deveined
- Lemongrass stalks
- 1 red chili pepper, seeded and chopped

Preparation:
1. Mix all the ingredients in a bowl except for the lemongrass and let them marinate for about 2 hours.
2. Preheat the oven to 390°F and lightly grease a baking dish.
3. Thread the shrimps onto the lemongrass stalks and place them in a single layer in the baking dish.
4. Bake for about 15 minutes in the preheated oven.

Serving Suggestions: Serve garnished with parsley.
Variation Tip: You can squeeze lemon juice on the shrimp before serving.
Nutritional Information per Serving:
Calories: 251|Fat: 10.3g|Sat Fat: 5.7g|Carbohydrates: 3g|Fiber: 0.2g|Sugar: 0.1g|Protein: 34.6g

Cumin-Crusted Fish Fillets

Prep Time: 10 minutes
Cook Time: 8 minutes
Servings: 4

Ingredients:
- 1 tablespoon ground cumin
- ¼ teaspoon thyme
- 1 teaspoon paprika
- ½ teaspoon lemon pepper
- 1-pound white fish fillets
- ½ tablespoon olive oil
- 2 tablespoons parsley, chopped
- Lemon or lime wedges

Preparation:

1. Mix the cumin, paprika, thyme, and lemon pepper in a small bowl.
2. Rub both sides of the fillets with the spice mixture.
3. Heat the olive oil in a large non-stick skillet and cook the fish fillets for about 4 minutes per side over medium heat.
4. Sprinkle the fillets with parsley and serve topped with lemon or lime wedges.

Serving Suggestions: Serve with a mint dip.
Variation Tip: You can use walleye, halibut, or cod for this recipe.
Nutritional Information per Serving:
Calories: 219|Fat: 10.7g|Sat Fat: 1.6g|Carbohydrates: 1.5g|Fiber: 0.6g|Sugar: 0.1g|Protein: 28.2g

Skillet Sea Scallops

Prep Time: 10 minutes
Cook Time: 10 minutes
Servings: 4

Ingredients:
- ½ teaspoon salt
- 2 tablespoons low-fat butter
- ½ cup dry breadcrumbs
- 1-pound sea scallops
- 1 tablespoon olive oil
- 2 tablespoons lemon juice
- 1 garlic clove, minced
- ¼ cup white wine
- 1 teaspoon fresh parsley, minced

Preparation:
1. Toss the breadcrumbs with the salt in a bowl.
2. Dredge the scallops in the mixture to coat evenly on both sides.
3. Put the butter and olive oil in a large skillet and cook the scallops for 2 minutes per side over medium-high heat.
4. Remove the scallops from the pan and keep them aside.
5. Put the wine, lemon juice, and garlic in the same skillet and let it reach a boil.
6. Add the parsley, then pour over the scallops to serve.

Serving Suggestions: Serve garnished with more fresh parsley.
Variation Tip: You can also use vegetable broth.
Nutritional Information per Serving:
Calories: 249|Fat: 11g|Sat Fat: 4g|Carbohydrates: 14g|Fiber: 1g|Sugar: 1g|Protein: 21g

Tomato Walnut Tilapia

Prep Time: 15 minutes
Cook Time: 9 minutes
Servings: 4
Ingredients:
- ¼ teaspoon salt
- 4 (4 ounces) tilapia fillets
- ¼ teaspoon black pepper
- 1 medium tomato, thinly sliced
- 1 tablespoon butter
Topping:
- ¼ cup walnuts, chopped
- ½ cup soft breadcrumbs
- 2 tablespoons lemon juice
- 1½ teaspoons butter, melted
Preparation:
1. Season the tilapia fillets with salt and black pepper.
2. Heat the butter in a large non-stick skillet and cook the fillets for 3 minutes per side over medium-high heat.
3. Move the tilapia fillets to a broiler pan and top with the tomato slices.
4. Mix the topping ingredients, then ladle the mixture over the tomato slices.
5. Broil for 3 minutes until lightly browned, then dish out to serve.
Serving Suggestions: Serve topped with walnuts.
Variation Tip: You can also use some red pepper flakes for spiciness.
Nutritional Information per Serving:
Calories: 202|Fat: 10g|Sat Fat: 4g|Carbohydrates: 6g|Fiber: 1g|Sugar: 2g|Protein: 23g

Shrimp Stir-Fry

Prep Time: 10 Minutes
Cook Time: 10 Minutes
Serves: 1
Ingredients:
- 1 tablespoon low-sodium soy sauce
- ¼ tablespoon balsamic vinegar
- 1 teaspoon erythritol
- ¼ tablespoon arrowroot starch
- ¼ tablespoon fresh ginger, minced
- ⅛ teaspoon red pepper flakes, crushed
- ½ tablespoon olive oil
- ½ small bell pepper, julienned
- ¼ small onion, julienned
- ¼ red chili, chopped
- ¼ pound shrimp, peeled and deveined
- ¼ scallion, chopped
Preparation:
1. Place the soy sauce, vinegar, erythritol, arrowroot starch, ginger, and red pepper flakes in a suitable bowl and mix well. Set aside.
2. Heat the oil in a small wok over high heat and stir-fry the bell peppers, onion, and red chili for almost 1–2 minutes.
3. Using a spoon, push the pepper mixture to the edge of the wok to create a space in the center.
4. Place the shrimp in a single layer in the center of the wok and cook for 1–2 minutes.
5. Stir the shrimp with the bell pepper mixture and cook for almost 2 minutes.
6. Stir in the sauce and cook for 2–3 minutes, stirring frequently.
7. Stir in the scallion and remove from the heat.
8. Serve hot.
Serving Suggestion: Garnish with chopped green onions.
Variation Tip: Omit the red pepper flakes for a milder dish.
Nutritional Information per Serving:
Calories 266 | Fat 9.7g | Sodium 865mg | Carbs 23.2g | Fiber 2.8g | Sugar 13.1g | Protein 28.9g

Diabetes-Friendly Lobster

Prep Time: 20 minutes
Cook Time: 3 minutes
Servings: 6

Ingredients:
- 1 teaspoon Old Bay Seasoning
- 1½ cups water
- 2 pounds fresh lobster tails
- ½ cup mayonnaise
- 2 tablespoons fresh lemon juice, divided
- 1 scallion, chopped
- 2 tablespoons unsalted butter, melted

Preparation:
1. Position the steamer trivet at the bottom of an Instant Pot, then add water and a pinch of Old Bay Seasoning.
2. Place the lobster tails, shell side down, on the trivet top.
3. Add 1 tablespoon of lemon juice over the lobster.
4. Secure the lid and cook on high pressure for about 3 minutes.
5. Quickly release the pressure and put the tails in an ice bath for about 1 minute.
6. Using kitchen scissors, cut the underside of the tails straight down the middle center.
7. Take out the meat and chop it into large chunks.
8. Mix the lobster meat, mayonnaise, scallions, butter, seasoning, and lemon juice in a large bowl and toss well before serving.

Serving Suggestions: Serve topped with lime wedges.

Variation Tip: You can add some cream cheese in the filling too.

Nutritional Information per Serving:
Calories: 247|Fat: 11.7g|Sat Fat: 3.7g|Carbohydrates: 5g|Fiber: 0.1g|Sugar: 1.4g|Protein: 29g

Roasted Vegetable Strata

Prep Time: 50 minutes plus overnight for marinating
Cook Time: 50 minutes
Servings: 8
Ingredients:
- 1 each: red, yellow, and orange bell peppers, cut into 1-inch pieces
- 3 large zucchinis, halved lengthwise and cut into ¾-inch slices
- 2 tablespoons olive oil
- ½ teaspoon salt
- ½ teaspoon dried basil
- 1 loaf (1-pound) crusty Italian bread, unsliced
- ½ cup Asiago cheese, shredded
- 2 cups fat-free milk
- 1 teaspoon dried oregano
- ½ teaspoon pepper
- 1 medium tomato, chopped
- ½ cup sharp cheddar cheese, shredded
- 6 large eggs

Preparation:
1. Preheat the oven to 400°F and lightly grease a baking pan and baking dish.
2. Toss the zucchini and red, yellow, and orange peppers with the olive oil and seasonings.
3. Transfer to the baking pan and roast for about 30 minutes in the preheated oven, stirring once.
4. Add the tomato and let everything cool slightly.
5. Layer half of the bread, roasted vegetables, and cheeses in the baking dish. Repeat layers.
6. Mix the eggs and milk in a bowl and pour the mixture evenly over the top of the bread-vegetable mixture.
7. Refrigerate overnight, then bake for about 50 minutes at 375°F.
8. Dish out and serve.
Serving Suggestions: Serve over couscous.
Variation Tip: You can make this recipe with turkey meat too.
Nutritional Information per Serving:
Calories: 349|Fat: 14g|Sat Fat: 5g|Carbohydrates: 40g|Fiber: 4g|Sugar: 9g|Protein: 17g

Lemony Brussels Sprouts

Prep Time: 10 Minutes
Cook Time: 18 Minutes
Serves: 4
Ingredients:
- 1-pound Brussels sprouts
- 2 tablespoons avocado oil, divided
- 1 cup chicken bone broth
- 1 tablespoon garlic, minced
- ½ teaspoon kosher salt
- Black pepper, to taste
- ½ medium lemon
- ½ tablespoon poppy seeds

Preparation:
1. Trim the Brussels sprouts by removing the loose outer leaves and cutting off the stem ends. Each one should be cut in half lengthwise (through the stem).
2. Select the "Sauté" setting on an electric pressure cooker.
3. Add 1 tablespoon of avocado oil to the cooker. Add half of the Brussels sprouts, cut-side down. Let them brown for 3–5 minutes without being stirred.
4. Transfer the sprouts to a bowl. Add the remaining tablespoon of avocado oil and Brussels sprouts to the same saucepan and repeat. Return all of the Brussels sprouts to the pot and cancel the "Sauté" setting.
5. Combine the broth, garlic, salt, and a few grinds of pepper in a mixing bowl. To evenly distribute the seasonings, give it a good stir. Add the mixture to the sprouts in the cooker.
6. Close and lock the lid. Set the valve to seal. Cook on high pressure for 2 minutes.
7. Zest the lemon and chop it into quarters while the Brussels sprouts cook. When the cooking is finished, release the pressure quickly.
8. Transfer the Brussels sprouts to a serving bowl with a slotted spoon.
9. Serve right away.
Serving Suggestion: Top with the poppy seeds, lemon zest, and a squeeze of lemon juice.
Variation Tip: Substitute Brussels sprouts with broccoli.
Nutritional Information per Serving:
Calories 126 | Fat 8.1g | Sodium 344mg | Carbs 12.9g | Fiber 4.9g | Sugar 3g | Protein 4.1g

Tofu Stir-Fry

Prep Time: 10 Minutes
Cook Time: 10 Minutes
Serves: 3

Ingredients:
• 9 ounces firm tofu, cubed
• 3 tablespoons low-sodium soy sauce
• 1 teaspoon sesame seeds
• 1 tablespoon sesame oil
• 1 cup spinach, chopped
• ¼ cup water

Preparation:
1. Combine the soy sauce and sesame oil in a mixing bowl.
2. Dip the tofu cubes in the soy sauce mixture and leave them for 10 minutes to marinate.
3. Heat a non-stick skillet and add the tofu cubes. (Keep the soy sauce mixture for later.) Cook the tofu cubes for 1½ minutes per side.
4. Add the water, the remaining soy sauce mixture, and chopped spinach.
5. Cover the skillet with a lid and cook for 5 minutes more.

Serving Suggestion: Top with sesame seeds.
Variation Tip: Replace sesame oil with olive oil.
Nutritional Information per Serving:
Calories 118 | Fat 8.6g | Sodium 406mg | Carbs 3.1g | Fiber 1.1g | Sugar 1.6g | Protein 8.5g

Cauliflower Fried Rice

Prep Time: 10 Minutes
Cook Time: 18 Minutes
Serves: 4

Ingredients:
• 1 tablespoon sesame oil
• 1 tablespoon garlic, minced
• 2 teaspoons fresh ginger, peeled and grated
• 8 cups riced cauliflower (fresh or frozen)
• 2 eggs, beaten
• 1 large carrot, shredded
• 2 cups frozen peas, thawed
• 2 tablespoons soy sauce
• 1 scallion, both white and green parts, thinly sliced
• 2 teaspoons sesame seeds

Preparation:

1. In a large pan, heat the oil over medium-high heat.
2. Sauté the garlic and ginger for about 2 minutes, until fragrant.
3. Add the cauliflower and carrot and cook for about 10 minutes, tossing until heated through and the liquid evaporates.
4. Add the peas and soy sauce and toss for about 4 minutes, or until mixed and the peas are warmed through.
5. Push the cauliflower rice to the side of the skillet and pour in the eggs.
6. Scramble the eggs for about 2 minutes, then mix them into the rice.
7. Serve and enjoy!

Serving Suggestion: Top with scallions and sesame seeds.
Variation Tip: Add chopped cooked chicken or shrimp instead of eggs to make it a complete meal.
Nutritional Information per Serving:
Calories 203 | Fat 8g | Sodium 373mg | Carbs 25g | Fiber 9g | Sugar 9g | Protein 12g

Vegetarian Black Bean Pasta

Prep Time: 5 minutes
Cook Time: 12 minutes
Servings: 6

Ingredients:
• 1 tablespoon olive oil
• 9 ounces whole-wheat fettuccine, cooked
• 1¾ cups baby Portobello mushrooms, sliced
• 1 can (15 ounces) black beans, drained
• 1 teaspoon dried rosemary, crushed
• 2 cups fresh baby spinach
• 1 garlic clove, minced
• 1 can (14½ ounces) diced tomatoes, undrained
• ½ teaspoon dried oregano

Preparation:
1. Heat the olive oil in a skillet over medium-high heat and cook the mushrooms for about 6 minutes.
2. Add the garlic and sauté for 1 minute.
3. Add the black beans, rosemary, tomatoes, and oregano and mix well.
4. Add the spinach and cook for about 5 minutes.
5. Stir in the fettuccine and toss well before serving.

Serving Suggestions: Serve alongside roasted vegetables.
Variation Tip: You can use any pasta of your choice.
Nutritional Information per Serving:
Calories: 255|Fat: 3g|Sat Fat: 0g|Carbohydrates: 45g|Fiber: 9g|Sugar: 4g|Protein: 12g

Lemon and Garlic Green Beans

Prep Time: 10 Minutes
Cook Time: 10 Minutes
Serves: 6
Ingredients:
- 1½ pounds green beans, trimmed
- 2 tablespoons olive oil
- 1 tablespoon fresh lemon juice
- 2 cloves garlic, minced
- Salt and pepper to taste

Preparation:
1. Boil the green beans in salted water.
2. Drain when done after 3 minutes and place them in ice-cold water. Cool the beans thoroughly, then drain them well.
3. Heat the oil in a large skillet over medium-high heat and add the blanched green beans.
4. Add the lemon juice, garlic, salt, and pepper and sauté for 3 minutes until the beans are tender-crisp, then serve hot.

Serving Suggestion: Top with sesame seeds.
Variation Tip: Add chili for a varied taste.
Nutritional Information per Serving:
Calories 75 | Fat 4.8g | Sodium 7mg | Carbs 8.5g | Fiber 3.9g | Sugar 1.7g | Protein 2.1g

Mashed Butternut Squash

Prep Time: 10 Minutes
Cook Time: 25 Minutes
Serves: 6
Ingredients:
- 3 pounds whole butternut squash (about 2 medium)
- 2 tablespoons olive oil
- Salt and pepper to taste

Preparation:
1. Preheat the oven to 400°F and line a baking sheet with parchment paper.
2. Cut the squash in half, peel it, and remove the seeds.
3. Cut the squash into cubes, grease it with some oil, and lay the cubes out evenly onto the prepared baking sheet.
4. Bake in the preheated oven for 25 minutes until tender, then place in a food processor. Add the olive oil.
5. Blend gently, then season with salt and pepper to taste.

Serving Suggestion: Garnish with rosemary sprigs.
Variation Tip: Substitute butternut squash with sweet potato.
Nutritional Information per Serving:
Calories 90 | Fat 4.8g | Sodium 5mg | Carbs 12g | Fiber 2g | Sugar 2.3g | Protein 1.1g

Mushroom Stroganoff

Prep Time: 10 Minutes
Cook Time: 20 Minutes
Serves: 4
Ingredients:
- 2 cups mushrooms, sliced
- 1 teaspoon whole-grain wheat flour
- 1 tablespoon olive oil
- 1 onion, chopped
- 1 teaspoon dried thyme
- 1 garlic clove, diced
- 1 teaspoon ground black pepper
- ½ cup soy milk

Preparation:
1. Heat the olive oil in a saucepan over medium-high heat.
2. Add the mushrooms and onion and cook them for 10 minutes. Stir the vegetables from time to time.
3. Season with ground black pepper, then add the thyme and garlic.
4. Add the soy milk and bring the mixture to a boil. Add the flour and stir the mixture until it's well combined.
5. Cook the mushroom stroganoff until it thickens.

Serving Suggestion: Garnish with fresh cilantro or parsley.
Variation Tip: Substitute soy milk with almond milk.
Nutritional Information per Serving:
Calories 70 | Fat 4.1g | Sodium 19mg | Carbs 6.9g | Fiber 1.5g | Sugar 3g | Protein 2.6g

Cranberry Cauliflower Roast

Prep Time: 10 Minutes
Cook Time: 25 Minutes
Serves: 4

Ingredients:
- 1 head cauliflower, cut into florets
- 2 tablespoons olive oil
- 1 tablespoon curry powder
- ¼ cup cranberries, dried
- ½ teaspoon Himalayan pink salt

Preparation:
1. Preheat the oven to 375°F
2. In a large mixing bowl, using your hands, mix the cauliflower florets and the olive oil until fully coated.
3. Mix in the curry powder, dried cranberries, and Himalayan pink salt and toss to combine.
4. Transfer the cauliflower mixture into a deep ovenproof dish. Bake in the preheated oven for 20–25 minutes until the cauliflower is fully cooked and lightly browned.

Serving Suggestion: Garnish with freshly chopped cilantro.

Variation Tip: Substitute cranberry with currants.

Nutritional Information per Serving:
Calories 100 | Fat 7.3g | Sodium 231mg | Carbs 5.1g | Fiber 2.4g | Sugar 1.9g | Protein 3g

Veggie Chili

Prep Time: 7 minutes
Cook Time: 43 minutes
Servings: 4

Ingredients:
- ½ tablespoon chili powder
- 1 garlic clove, minced
- 8 ounces canned kidney beans, rinsed and drained
- 7 ounces tomato sauce
- ½ tablespoon olive oil

- 2 carrots, sliced
- ½ zucchini, chopped
- 8 ounces canned black beans, rinsed and drained
- 7 ounces canned no-salt-added tomatoes, in juice, diced
- ½ medium onion, chopped
- ½ green bell pepper, chopped

Preparation:
1. In a large pot, cook the onion, carrots, green pepper, and zucchini in olive oil for about 7 minutes over medium-high heat.
2. Add the garlic and sauté for 30 seconds.
3. Add the remaining ingredients and let the mixture reach a boil.
4. Secure the lid, reduce the heat, and simmer for about 35 minutes.
5. Dish out, serve, and enjoy!

Serving Suggestions: Serve with rice.

Variation Tip: You can add crushed red chilies to add some spice to it.

Nutritional Information per Serving:
Calories: 361|Fat: 2.9g|Sat Fat: 0.4g|Carbohydrates: 65.4g|Fiber: 16.4g|Sugar: 7.3g|Protein: 21.7g

Tofu with Mushrooms

Prep Time: 5 minutes
Cook Time: 9 minutes
Servings: 6

Ingredients:
- 8 tablespoons parmesan cheese, shredded
- 2 cups fresh mushrooms, finely chopped
- 2 blocks tofu, pressed and cubed into 1-inch pieces
- Salt and black pepper, to taste
- 8 tablespoons butter

Preparation:
1. Season the tofu with salt and black pepper in a bowl.
2. Heat the butter in a pan, add the seasoned tofu, and cook for about 5 minutes over medium-low heat.
3. Add the parmesan cheese and mushrooms and cook for about 4 minutes, occasionally stirring.
4. Dish out and serve hot.

Serving Suggestions: Serve topped with green onions.

Variation Tip: You can use cremini or button mushrooms.

Nutritional Information per Serving:
Calories: 211|Fat: 18.5g|Sat Fat: 11.5g|Carbohydrates: 2g|Fiber: 0.4g|Sugar: 0.5g|Protein: 11.5g

Endive and Sweet Potato Bake

Prep Time: 10 Minutes
Cook Time: 45 Minutes
Serves: 4

Ingredients:
• Non-stick cooking spray
• 2 endives, leaves separated and divided
• 2 orange sweet potatoes, peeled and thinly sliced
• Black pepper, to taste
• 1 tablespoon fennel seeds, ground
• ½ teaspoon cinnamon, ground
• ¼ teaspoon nutmeg, ground
• 1 cup vegetable broth

Preparation:
1. Heat the oven to 375°F
2. Prepare a deep baking dish by coating it with non-stick cooking spray.
3. Cover the bottom of the baking dish with half the endive leaves and layer half the thinly sliced sweet potatoes on top.
4. Sprinkle the ground black pepper, ground fennel seeds, and half the ground cinnamon and ground nutmeg on top of the potatoes.
5. Continue to do this for the subsequent few layers until all the endive leaves, sliced sweet potatoes, ground cinnamon, ground fennel seeds, and ground nutmeg is used.
6. Add the vegetable broth and cover the deep baking dish with aluminum foil.
7. Bake in the preheated oven for 45 minutes until the vegetables are tender.
8. Serve hot.

Serving Suggestion: Garnish with fresh cilantro.
Variation Tip: You can use white sweet potatoes or yams for this recipe. You can also replace the endives with 1 sliced fennel bulb.

Nutritional Information per Serving:
Calories 153 | Fat 2g | Sodium 284mg | Carbs 23g | Fiber 10.7g | Sugar 3.6g | Protein 5.7g

Tomato and Avocado Sandwiches

Prep Time: 10 minutes
Cook Time: 0 minutes

Servings: 2
Ingredients:
• 4 slices whole-wheat bread, toasted
• ½ medium ripe avocado, peeled and mashed
• 1 medium tomato, sliced
• ¼ cup hummus
• 2 tablespoons shallot, finely chopped

Preparation:
1. Spread 2 slices of toast with mashed avocado.
2. Add the tomato and shallot on top.
3. Layer hummus on the remaining bread slices.
4. Place each slice of avocado toast on top of a slice of hummus toast and serve.

Serving Suggestions: Serve with vegetable crisps.
Variation Tip: You can add some red chili flakes to the mashed avocado for heat.

Nutritional Information per Serving:
Calories: 278|Fat: 11g|Sat Fat: 2g|Carbohydrates: 35g|Fiber: 9g|Sugar: 6g|Protein: 11g

Spaghetti Squash

Prep Time: 10 Minutes
Cook Time: 1 Hour
Serves: 4

Ingredients:
• 2 pounds spaghetti squash, cut lengthwise
• Sea salt and black pepper, to taste
• 3 tablespoons olive oil, divided
• 1 tablespoon fresh basil, finely diced
• 1 tablespoon fresh parsley, finely diced
• 1 tablespoon fresh rosemary, finely diced
• 2 teaspoons garlic, minced
• ¼ cup vegan parmesan cheese, grated, for serving

Preparation:
1. Preheat the oven to 400°F and use aluminum foil to cover a baking sheet.
2. Season the halved spaghetti squash with ground sea salt and ground black pepper and drizzle it with 1 tablespoon of olive oil.
3. Put the spaghetti squash, cut side down, on the baking sheet, and bake for 50–60 minutes, until tender. Let it cool for a few minutes when it's done.
4. Use a fork to scrape the spaghetti squash strands into a large serving bowl. Add the remaining 2 tablespoons of olive oil, basil, parsley, rosemary, and garlic, and combine.
5. Season with ground sea salt and ground black pepper.
6. Serve.

Serving Suggestion: Top with the grated vegan parmesan cheese.
Variation Tip: You can use julienned courgettes in place of the spaghetti squash.

Nutritional Information per Serving:
Calories 186 | Fat 13.3g | Sodium 125mg | Carbs 16.9g | Fiber 0.4g | Sugar 0g | Protein 3.5g

Pan-Roasted Broccoli

Prep Time: 10 Minutes
Cook Time: 10 Minutes
Serves: 6

Ingredients:
- ¼ teaspoon salt
- ⅛ teaspoon pepper
- 2 tablespoons extra-virgin olive oil
- 1¾ pounds broccoli, florets cut into 1½-inch pieces, stalks peeled and cut into ¼-inch-thick slices

Preparation:
1. Stir 3 tablespoons of water, salt, and pepper together in a small bowl until the salt dissolves; set aside.
2. Heat the oil in a 12-inch non-stick skillet over medium-high heat until just smoking.
3. Add the broccoli stalks in an even layer and cook, without stirring, until browned on the bottom, about 2 minutes. Add the florets to the skillet and toss to combine.
4. Cook, without stirring, until the bottoms of the florets just begin to brown, 1–2 minutes.
5. Add the water mixture and cover the skillet.
6. Cook until the broccoli is bright green but still crisp, about 2 minutes.
7. Uncover and cook until the water evaporates, the broccoli stalks are tender, and the florets are crisp-tender, about 2 minutes.
8. Serve.

Serving Suggestion: Top with pepper flakes.
Variation Tip: You can replace broccoli with zucchini.
Nutritional Information per Serving:
Calories 126 | Fat 5.5g | Sodium 178mg | Carbs 17g | Fiber 6.7g | Sugar 4.2g | Protein 7g

Roasted Beans and Green Onions

Prep Time: 10 Minutes
Cook Time: 10 Minutes
Serves: 4

Ingredients:
- 8 ounces green string beans, trimmed
- 4 whole green onions, trimmed and cut in fourths (about 3-inch pieces)
- 1½ teaspoons extra-virgin olive oil
- ¼ teaspoon salt

Preparation:
1. Preheat the oven to 425°F. Line a baking sheet with foil and coat the foil with non-stick cooking spray.
2. Toss the beans, onions, and oil together in a medium bowl.
3. Arrange them in a thin layer on the prepared baking sheet.
4. Bake for 7 minutes in the preheated oven, then stir gently, using two utensils as you would for a stir-fry.
5. Bake for another 3–4 minutes or until the beans begin to brown on the edges and are tender-crisp.
6. Remove from the oven and sprinkle the beans with salt.

Serving Suggestion: Serve with lemon slices.
Variation Tip: Feel free to add more seasoning.
Nutritional Information per Serving:
Calories 35 | Fat 1.9g | Sodium 153mg | Carbs 5.1g | Fiber 2.3g | Sugar 1.1g | Protein 1.3g

Portobello Polenta Stacks

Prep Time: 15 minutes
Cook Time: 27 minutes
Servings: 4

Ingredients:
- 3 garlic cloves, minced
- 1 tablespoon olive oil
- 2 tablespoons balsamic vinegar
- ¼ teaspoon salt
- 1 tube (18 ounces) polenta, cut into 12 slices
- ½ cup parmesan cheese, grated
- 4 large Portobello mushrooms, stems removed
- ¼ teaspoon pepper
- 4 slices tomato
- 2 tablespoons fresh basil, minced

Preparation:
1. Preheat the oven to 400°F and lightly grease a baking dish.
2. Heat the olive oil in a saucepan and sauté the garlic for 2 minutes over medium heat.
3. Stir in the vinegar, then remove from the heat.
4. Put the mushrooms in the prepared baking dish and sprinkle with the vinegar mixture, salt, and black pepper.
5. Top with the polenta, tomato slices, and parmesan cheese.
6. Bake for about 25 minutes in the preheated oven, uncovered, and dish out.

Serving Suggestions: Serve sprinkled with fresh basil.
Variation Tip: You can also serve over quinoa.
Nutritional Information per Serving:
Calories: 219|Fat: 6g|Sat Fat: 2g|Carbohydrates: 32g|Fiber: 3g|Sugar: 7g|Protein: 7g

Golden Beet and Peach Soup With Tarragon

Prep Time: 20 minutes
Cook Time: 45 minutes
Servings: 6
Ingredients:
• 1 tablespoon olive oil
• 2 pounds fresh golden beets, peeled and cut into 1-inch cubes
• 2 cups white grape-peach juice
• ¼ cup plain Greek yogurt
• 2 medium fresh peaches, peeled and diced
• 2 tablespoons cider vinegar
• ¼ teaspoon fresh tarragon, finely chopped
• Fresh tarragon sprigs
Preparation:
1. Preheat the oven to 400°F and lightly grease a baking pan.
2. Arrange the beets in the baking pan and drizzle with olive oil.
3. Roast for about 45 minutes in the preheated oven.
4. Put the cooked beets in a blender and add the grape-peach juice and cider vinegar.
5. Blend well, then refrigerate for 1 hour.
6. Mix the Greek yogurt and chopped tarragon in a small bowl, then refrigerate.
7. Arrange the beet mixture in serving bowls and spoon the Greek yogurt mixture over them.
8. Top with peaches and tarragon sprigs before serving.
Serving Suggestions: Serve with your favorite salad on the side.
Variation Tip: You can substitute ½ teaspoon chopped fresh thyme, fresh chives, or fresh basil for the tarragon.
Nutritional Information per Serving:
Calories: 159|Fat: 4g|Sat Fat: 1g|Carbohydrates: 31g|Fiber: 4g|Sugar: 26g|Protein: 3g

Cheesy Cauli Bake

Prep Time: 10 Minutes
Cook Time: 30 Minutes
Serves: 6

Ingredients:
• 3 tablespoons tahini
• 2 tablespoons nutritional yeast
• 1 tablespoon lemon juice
• ½ teaspoon pure maple syrup
• ½ teaspoon sea salt
• ½ cup + 1 tablespoon plain non-dairy milk
• 3½ cups cauliflower florets, cut or broken into small pieces
Topping
• 1 tablespoon almond meal or breadcrumbs
• ½ tablespoons nutritional yeast
• Pinch of sea salt
Preparation:
1. Preheat the oven to 425°F.
2. Use cooking spray to lightly coat the bottom and sides of an 8-inch x 8-inch (or similar size) baking dish.
3. Whisk the tahini, nutritional yeast, lemon juice, maple syrup or agave nectar, and salt in a small bowl. Gradually whisk in the milk until it all comes together smoothly.
4. In the baking dish, add the cauliflower and pour in the sauce; stir thoroughly to coat the cauliflower.
5. Cover with foil and bake in the preheated oven for 25–30 minutes, stirring only once, until the cauliflower is tender.
6. In a small bowl, toss together the topping ingredients.
7. Remove the foil from the cauliflower, and sprinkle on the topping. Return to the oven and set the oven to broil.
8. Allow it to broil for a minute until the topping is golden brown.
9. Remove, let it sit for a few minutes, then serve.
Serving Suggestion: Garnish with fresh cilantro.
Variation Tip: You can use agave nectar in place of maple syrup.
Nutritional Information per Serving:
Calories 139 | Fat 4.9g | Sodium 186mg | Carbs 19.3g | Fiber 8.4g | Sugar 7.4g | Protein 9.1g

Creamy Fettuccine with Brussels Sprouts and Mushrooms

Prep Time: 10 minutes
Cook Time: 25 minutes
Servings: 6
Ingredients:
• 1 tablespoon extra-virgin olive oil
• 12 ounces whole-wheat fettuccine
• 4 cups mixed mushrooms, sliced
• 1 tablespoon garlic, minced
• 2 tablespoons all-purpose flour
• ½ teaspoon freshly ground pepper

- 4 cups Brussels sprouts, thinly sliced
- ½ cup dry sherry
- 2 cups low-fat milk
- ½ teaspoon salt
- 1 cup Asiago cheese, finely shredded

Preparation:
1. Fill a pot with water and let it reach a boil.
2. Add the pasta and cook for about 10 minutes. Drain well and keep aside.
3. Meanwhile, put the olive oil in a large skillet and cook the mushrooms and Brussels sprouts for about 10 minutes over medium heat, stirring often.
4. Add the garlic and sauté for 1 minute, stirring thoroughly.
5. Add the dry sherry and let it reach a boil.
6. Cook for 1 minute, stirring often.
7. Whisk the milk and flour in a bowl, then add the mixture to the skillet with salt and black pepper.
8. Cook for about 2 minutes and stir in the Asiago cheese.
9. Drizzle the sauce over the cooked pasta and toss gently before serving.

Serving Suggestions: Serve with more cheese, if desired.

Variation Tip: You can also use sherry vinegar instead of dry sherry.

Nutritional Information per Serving:
Calories: 384|Fat: 10.2g|Sat Fat: 4.4g|Carbohydrates: 56.4g|Fiber: 96g|Sugar: 8.4g|Protein: 18.4g

Chili-Lime Mushroom Tacos

Prep Time: 5 minutes
Cook Time: 8 minutes
Servings: 4

Ingredients:
- 1 tablespoon olive oil
- 1 medium onion, halved and thinly sliced
- 4 large Portobello mushrooms, sliced
- 1 medium sweet red pepper, cut into strips
- 2 garlic cloves, minced
- ½ teaspoon salt
- ¼ teaspoon red pepper flakes, crushed
- 2 tablespoons lime juice
- 1 cup pepper jack cheese, shredded
- 1½ teaspoons chili powder
- ½ teaspoon ground cumin
- 1 teaspoon lime zest, grated
- 8 corn tortillas (6-inch), warmed

Preparation:

1. Heat the olive oil in a skillet over medium-high heat and sauté the mushrooms, red pepper, and onion for about 7 minutes.
2. Stir in the seasonings, garlic, lime zest, and lime juice. Cook for 1 minute, stirring well.
3. Add this mixture to the tortillas and top with cheese before serving.

Serving Suggestions: Serve with your favorite pasta or rice.

Variation Tip: You can use lemon juice and zest too.

Nutritional Information per Serving:
Calories: 300|Fat: 14g|Sat Fat: 6g|Carbohydrates: 33g|Fiber: 6g|Sugar: 5g|Protein: 13g

Chopped Greek Salad

Prep Time: 15 minutes
Cook Time: 0 minutes
Servings: 4

Ingredients:

Salad:
- 4 cups romaine, chopped
- 1 can (15 ounces) garbanzo beans or chickpeas, rinsed and drained
- 2 celery ribs, sliced
- 1 medium tomato, chopped
- ⅓ cup Greek olives, sliced
- ⅓ cup feta cheese, crumbled
- ¼ cup pepperoncini, finely chopped

Dressing:
- 2 tablespoons pepperoncini juice
- 2 tablespoons fresh basil, minced
- 2 tablespoons extra-virgin olive oil
- ¼ teaspoon salt
- 1 tablespoon lemon juice
- ¼ teaspoon black pepper

Preparation:
1. Mix all the dressing ingredients in a small bowl.
2. Place the salad ingredients in a large bowl.
3. Drizzle the dressing over the salad and mix well before serving.

Serving Suggestions: Serve with roasted veggies.

Variation Tip: Replace the feta cheese with toasted pine nuts.

Nutritional Information per Serving:
Calories: 235|Fat: 14g|Sat Fat: 2g|Carbohydrates: 22g|Fiber: 6g|Sugar: 4g|Protein: 7g

Stir-Fry Rice Bowl

Prep Time: 15 minutes
Cook Time: 15 minutes
Servings: 4

Ingredients:
- 2 medium carrots, julienned
- 1 tablespoon olive oil
- 1 medium zucchini, julienned
- 1 cup bean sprouts
- 1 tablespoon water
- 1 tablespoon chili garlic sauce
- 3 cups hot cooked brown rice
- ½ cup sliced baby portobello mushrooms
- 1 cup fresh baby spinach
- 1 tablespoon reduced-sodium soy sauce
- 4 large eggs, cold
- 1 teaspoon sesame oil

Preparation:
1. Put the olive oil in a skillet and cook the carrots, zucchini, and mushrooms for about 5 minutes over medium-high heat.
2. Add the bean sprouts, spinach, water, soy sauce, and chili sauce and cook for about 5 minutes.
3. Remove from the heat and keep aside.
4. Fill a saucepan halfway with water and let it reach a boil, then maintain a gentle simmer by adjusting the heat.
5. Crack one egg into a small bowl. Hold the bowl close to the water's surface and gently lower the egg into it.
6. Cook for about 5 minutes, uncovered, then remove the cooked egg from the water with a slotted spoon. Repeat with the remaining eggs.
7. Serve the rice in bowls and top with the vegetables.
8. Drizzle with sesame oil and top each serving with a poached egg.

Serving Suggestions: Serve topped with thyme sprigs.

Variation Tip: You can also use vegetable broth.

Nutritional Information per Serving:
Calories: 305|Fat: 11g|Sat Fat: 2g|Carbohydrates: 40g|Fiber: 4g|Sugar: 4g|Protein: 12g

Cumin Quinoa Patties

Prep Time: 15 minutes
Cook Time: 23 minutes
Servings: 4

Ingredients:
- ½ cup quinoa, rinsed
- 1 cup water
- 1 medium carrot, cut into 1-inch pieces
- ¼ cup panko breadcrumbs
- 1 large egg, lightly beaten
- ¼ teaspoon salt
- 2 tablespoons olive oil
- 1 cup canned cannellini beans, drained
- 3 green onions, chopped
- 3 teaspoons ground cumin
- ⅛ teaspoon pepper

Preparation:
1. Let the water reach a boil in a saucepan, then add the quinoa.
2. Reduce the heat to low, secure the lid, and simmer for about 15 minutes.
3. Remove the pan from the heat and fluff the quinoa with a fork.
4. Meanwhile, put the carrots and beans in a food processor and pulse until chopped coarsely.
5. Transfer the mixture to a large bowl and add the cooked quinoa, green onions, breadcrumbs, egg, and seasonings. Mix well.
6. Shape the mixture into patties.
7. Heat the olive oil in a skillet and cook the patties for 4 minutes per side over medium heat, turning carefully.
8. Dish out, drain on paper towels, and serve.

Serving Suggestions: Serve with any low-carb dip of your choice.

Variation Tip: You can use red beans in this recipe too.

Nutritional Information per Serving:
Calories: 235|Fat: 10g|Sat Fat: 1g|Carbohydrates: 28g|Fiber: 5g|Sugar: 2g|Protein: 8g

Zucchini and Tomato Stew

Prep Time: 10 Minutes
Cook Time: 20 Minutes
Serves: 5

Ingredients:
- 1 tablespoon plant-based butter
- 2 medium white onions, diced
- 3 cups zucchini, trimmed and sliced
- 2½ cups medium tomatoes, chopped
- 1 teaspoon Cajun seasoning

Preparation:
1. In a large cast-iron pan, melt the plant-based butter over medium heat.
2. Add the diced onion and fry until translucent and lightly browned.
3. Add the sliced zucchini and fry for 5 minutes, until browned.
4. Mix the chopped tomatoes and Cajun seasoning, then add to the pan. Cook for 10 minutes until the zucchini is tender and the tomatoes have broken down.

Serving Suggestion: Garnish with fresh cilantro.
Variation Tip: Feel free to add more seasoning.
Nutritional Information per Serving:
Calories 87 | Fat 3g | Sodium 47mg | Carbs 13g | Fiber 6.8g | Sugar 13.2g | Protein 3g

Chicken Dill Soup

Prep Time: 10 Minutes
Cook Time: 45 Minutes
Serves: 5

Ingredients:
- 1-pound skinless, boneless chicken breast, chopped
- 1 cup carrot, shredded
- 5 cups water

- 1 cup yellow onion, chopped
- 1 teaspoon smoked paprika
- ½ teaspoon chili powder
- ½ cup fresh dill, chopped

Preparation:
1. Put the chicken in a large pot.
2. Add all the remaining ingredients except the dill.
3. Cook the soup over medium heat for 40 minutes.
4. Serve hot.

Serving Suggestion: Garnish with the fresh chopped dill.
Variation Tip: Substitute water with chicken broth.
Nutritional Information per Serving:
Calories 136 | Fat 2.6g | Sodium 82mg | Carbs 7.4g | Fiber 1.9g | Sugar 2.1g | Protein 20.7g

Broccoli and Asparagus Soup

Prep Time: 10 Minutes
Cook Time: 20 Minutes
Serves: 6

Ingredients:
- 2 cups broccoli florets, chopped
- 15 asparagus spears, ends chopped
- 1 teaspoon dried oregano
- 1 tablespoon thyme leaves
- ½ cup unsweetened almond milk
- 3½ cups water
- 2 cups cauliflower florets, chopped
- 2 teaspoons garlic, chopped
- 1 cup onion, chopped
- 2 tablespoons olive oil
- Salt and black pepper, to taste

Preparation:
1. Add the oil to an Instant Pot and set it to "Sauté" mode.
2. Add the onion and sauté until softened.
3. Add the garlic and sauté for almost 30 seconds. Add all the vegetables and water and stir well.
4. Cover the pot with the lid and select to pressure cook for 3 minutes.
5. When finished, allow the pressure to release naturally, then open the lid.
6. Blend the soup using an immersion blender until smooth. Stir in the almond milk, herbs, pepper, and salt.
7. Serve fresh.

Serving Suggestion: Serve with whole-grain bread.
Variation Tip: Substitute water with broth.
Nutritional Information per Serving:
Calories 85 | Fat 10g | Sodium 42mg | Carbs 8.8g | Fiber 2g | Sugar 1g | Protein 3.3g

Turkey Chowder

Prep Time: 10 Minutes
Cook Time: 20 Minutes
Serves: 2

Ingredients:
- ½ cup ground turkey
- ¼ cup leek, chopped
- 1 teaspoon dried rosemary
- 1 cup water
- 1 cup plain yogurt
- 1 teaspoon olive oil

Preparation:
1. Cook the ground turkey with the olive oil in a pan for 10 minutes over medium-high heat. Stir well.
2. Add all the remaining ingredients and cover with a lid.
3. Cook the chowder for 10 minutes more on medium heat.

Serving Suggestion: Garnish with chopped green onions.
Variation Tip: Substitute ground turkey with ground chicken.
Nutritional Information per Serving:
Calories 277 | Fat 13g | Sodium 180mg | Carbs 10.6g | Fiber 0.5g | Sugar 9.1g | Protein 29.8g

Tarragon Soup

Prep Time: 10 Minutes
Cook Time: 10 Minutes
Serves: 2

Ingredients:
- 1 tablespoon avocado oil
- ½ cup onion, diced
- 3 garlic cloves, crushed
- Salt and black pepper, to taste
- 1 (13½-ounce) can full-fat coconut milk
- 1 tablespoon lemon juice
- ½ cup raw cashews
- 1 celery stalk

- 2 tablespoons fresh tarragon, chopped

Preparation:
1. In a skillet over medium heat, heat the avocado oil.
2. Add the onion, garlic, salt, and pepper, and sauté for 3–5 minutes or until the onion is soft.
3. In a high-speed blender, blend the coconut milk, lemon juice, cashews, celery, and tarragon with the onion mixture until smooth.
4. Adjust the seasonings, if necessary.
5. Serve and enjoy immediately, or transfer to a medium saucepan and warm on low heat for 3–5 minutes before serving.

Serving Suggestion: Garnish with fresh cilantro.
Variation Tip: Replace avocado oil with olive oil.
Nutritional Information per Serving:
Calories 60 | Fat 2g | Sodium 32mg | Carbs 13g | Fiber 2g | Sugar 4.3g | Protein 0.8g

Carrot Mushrooms Soup

Prep Time: 10 Minutes
Cook Time: 20 Minutes
Serves: 2

Ingredients:
- 4 carrots, peeled and cubed
- 4 potatoes, peeled and cubed
- 10 large mushrooms
- ½ white onion
- 2 tablespoons olive oil
- 3 cups vegetable stock
- 2 tablespoons fresh parsley
- Salt and white pepper, to taste

Preparation:
1. Wash and peel the carrots and potatoes, then dice them.
2. Heat the vegetable stock in a pot over medium heat.
3. Cook the carrots and potatoes in the pot for around 15 minutes.
4. Meanwhile, slice the onion and cook them in a heated non-stick skillet with the olive oil for around 3 minutes.
5. Wash the mushrooms, cut them into the desired size slices, and add to the skillet, cooking for 5 minutes, stirring occasionally. Add to the pot when done.
6. Add the carrots and potatoes to the pot.
7. Season with parsley, salt, and pepper. Cover with a lid and cook until the vegetables are tender.
8. Serve hot.

Serving Suggestion: Garnish with fresh rosemary.
Variation Tip: Substitute vegetable stock with chicken stock.
Nutritional Information per Serving:
Calories 75 | Fat 1.8g | Sodium 74mg | Carbs 13g | Fiber 2g | Sugar 1g | Protein 1g

White Mushroom Soup

Prep Time: 10 Minutes
Cook Time: 30 Minutes
Serves: 4

Ingredients:
- 4 cups water
- 1 yellow onion, chopped
- 1 tablespoon olive oil
- 8 ounces skinless, boneless chicken breast, chopped
- ½ pound white mushrooms, chopped
- 1 chili pepper, chopped
- 2 tablespoons yogurt

Preparation:
1. Heat a pot with the oil over medium heat. Add the onion, chilies, chicken breast, and mushrooms, and cook for 10 minutes, stirring occasionally.
2. Add all the remaining ingredients and cook the soup for 20 minutes.
3. Let the cooked soup rest for 10 minutes before serving.

Serving Suggestion: Garnish with fresh cilantro.
Variation Tip: Substitute chicken with turkey.
Nutritional Information per Serving:
Calories 124 | Fat 5.2g | Sodium 46mg | Carbs 5.1g | Fiber 1.2g | Sugar 2.7g | Protein 14.6g

Creamy Coconut Chicken Soup

Prep Time: 10 Minutes
Cook Time: 20 Minutes
Serves: 4

Ingredients:
- 1 tablespoon coconut oil
- 1 onion, chopped
- 1 red bell pepper, seeded and chopped
- 2 teaspoons garlic, minced
- 2 teaspoons fresh ginger, peeled and grated
- 3 cups low-sodium chicken broth
- 1 (13½-ounce) can light coconut milk
- 1 sweet potato, peeled and chopped
- 2 cups cooked rotisserie chicken, chopped
- 1 lime

Preparation:
1. Heat the oil over medium-high heat in a large stockpot and sauté the onion, bell pepper, garlic, and ginger for about 5 minutes until softened.

2. Add the broth, coconut milk, sweet potato, chicken, lime juice, and lime zest and bring to a boil.
3. Reduce the heat to low and simmer for 15 minutes until the sweet potatoes are tender.
4. Serve hot.

Serving Suggestion: Top the soup with chopped cilantro.
Variation Tip: You can also make it without the chicken and just add extra veggies or chickpeas. You can also use leftover turkey or chicken from another recipe.
Nutritional Information per Serving:
Calories 347 | Fat 19g | Sodium 142mg | Carbs 18g | Fiber 3g | Sugar 4g | Protein 26g

Slow Cooker Mediterranean Stew

Prep Time: 30 minutes
Cook Time: 10 hours
Servings: 10

Ingredients:
- 2 cups unpeeled eggplant, cubed
- 1 butternut squash, peeled, seeded, and cubed
- 2 cups zucchini, cubed
- 1 (8-ounce) can tomato sauce
- 1 ripe tomato, chopped
- ½ cup vegetable broth
- ½ teaspoon ground turmeric
- ¼ teaspoon ground cinnamon
- 1 (10-ounce) package frozen okra, thawed
- 1 cup onions, chopped
- 1 carrot, thinly sliced
- 1 garlic clove, chopped
- ½ teaspoon ground cumin
- ¼ teaspoon red pepper, crushed
- ¼ teaspoon paprika

Preparation:
1. Put the zucchini, butternut squash, eggplant, okra, onion, tomato sauce, tomato, broth, carrot, and garlic in a slow cooker. Mix well.
2. Season with the turmeric, cumin powder, red pepper, paprika, and cinnamon.
3. Secure the lid and cook on low pressure for 10 hours.
4. Dish out and serve hot.

Serving Suggestions: You can serve this dish with mashed potatoes.
Variation Tip: You can use veggies of your choice.
Nutritional Information per Serving:
Calories: 40|Fat: 0.3g|Sat Fat: 0.1g|Carbohydrates: 8.4g|Fiber: 2.8g|Sugar: 3.6g|Protein: 1.9g

Creamy Tomato Soup

Prep Time: 3 minutes
Cook Time: 2 minutes
Servings: 3

Ingredients:
- ⅔ cup no-salt-added canned tomato puree
- 2 tablespoons reduced-fat cream cheese
- ½ cup low-sodium chicken broth

Preparation:
1. Mix the puree, broth, and cream cheese in a large microwave-safe mug. Combine well.
2. Place the mug in the microwave and cook on high power for about 2 minutes, occasionally stirring.
3. Serve and enjoy!

Serving Suggestions: Serve topped with mint leaves.
Variation Tip: You can also use vegetable broth.
Nutritional Information per Serving:
Calories: 73|Fat: 2.6g|Sat Fat: 1.5g|Carbohydrates: 11.6g|Fiber: 2.4g|Sugar: 6.1g|Protein: 2.9g

Strawberry-Lemon Thyme Soup

Prep Time: 25 minutes
Cook Time: 0 minutes
Servings: 8

Ingredients:
- 2 cups low-fat buttermilk
- 6 cups fresh strawberries, sliced
- 4 teaspoons lemon peel, finely shredded
- 4 tablespoons honey
- 2 teaspoons fresh thyme, chopped

Preparation:
1. Put the strawberries and buttermilk in a blender. Blend well.
2. Transfer the mixture to a bowl and fold in the lemon peel and thyme.

3. Cover the bowl and chill the mixture for 30 minutes.
4. Strain the soup and discard the lemon peel and thyme.
5. Drizzle in honey and ladle out the chilled soup into serving bowls.

Serving Suggestions: Serve topped with mint leaves and chopped strawberries.
Variation Tip: You can also add basil to this soup.
Nutritional Information per Serving:
Calories: 92|Fat: 0.9g|Sat Fat: 0.4g|Carbohydrates: 20.3g|Fiber: 2.3g|Sugar: 16.9g|Protein: 2.8g

Tuscany Bean Soup

Prep Time: 5 minutes
Cook Time: 15 minutes
Servings: 3

Ingredients:
- ¼ teaspoon thyme
- 2 garlic cloves, crushed
- ½ teaspoon oregano
- 1½ cups tinned borlotti beans, drained
- 1 teaspoon pesto
- ½ onion, chopped
- ½ carrot, diced
- 1 cup tomatoes, chopped
- 1 tablespoon olive oil
- ½ yellow bell pepper, chopped
- 1½ cups gluten-free vegetable stock
- 1 cabbage leaf, chopped

Preparation:
1. Heat the oil in a pan, then add the onion, yellow pepper, and carrot. Cook for about 5 minutes over medium heat.
2. Add the vegetable stock, tomatoes, oregano, thyme, cabbage, and beans. Let the mixture reach a boil.
3. Reduce the heat and allow the mixture to simmer for 10 minutes.
4. Ladle the soup out into bowls. Sprinkle generously with black pepper and pesto before serving.

Serving Suggestions: Serve with garlic bread.
Variation Tip: You can add red beans too.
Nutritional Information per Serving:
Calories: 97|Fat: 5.9g|Sat Fat: 0.9g|Carbohydrates: 10.6g|Fiber: 3.3g|Sugar: 4.9g|Protein: 2.6g

Kale and Cauliflower Soup

Prep Time: 10 Minutes
Cook Time: 30 Minutes
Serves: 4
Ingredients:
• 2 tablespoons avocado oil
• 8 ounces green beans, cut into pieces
• 10 ounces cauliflower, cut into florets
• 1 tablespoon garlic, minced
• 8 cups vegetable stock
• 1 can tomatoes, diced
• 2 cups kale, chopped
• Sea salt and black pepper, to taste
• 1 tablespoon fresh parsley, chopped (optional)
• 1 tablespoon fresh cilantro, chopped (optional)
• 1 tablespoon chive, chopped (optional)
• ½ lemon, juice (optional)
Preparation:
1. Heat the avocado oil in a large pot over medium heat.
2. Add the cut green beans and cauliflower florets and cook for 7–9 minutes, occasionally stirring, until lightly browned.
3. Add the minced garlic and cook for 2 minutes, stirring occasionally.
4. Increase the heat to high, add the vegetable stock, diced tomatoes, and chopped kale. Bring the mixture to a boil.
5. Reduce the heat to low and let the mixture simmer gently for 15–20 minutes until the vegetables are tender.
6. Season with ground sea salt and ground black pepper.
7. Serve.
Serving Suggestion: Serve with a sprinkle of fresh parsley, cilantro, chives, and lemon juice (if using) for extra flavor.
Variation Tip: For more flavor, you can add cumin.
Nutritional Information per Serving:
Calories 94 | Fat 5.1g | Sodium 166mg | Carbs 19g | Fiber 5.4g | Sugar 7.8g | Protein 14g

Chicken and Mushroom Stew

Prep Time: 5 minutes
Cook Time: 16 minutes
Servings: 3
Ingredients:
• ½ small onion, chopped
• 4 (2½-ounce each) skinless chicken thighs
• ½ pound fresh cremini mushrooms, stemmed and quartered
• 1 cup fresh cherry tomatoes
• ½ cup fresh parsley, chopped
• ½ tablespoon tomato paste
• Black pepper, to taste
• 1 garlic clove, minced
• ¼ cup low-sodium chicken broth
• ½ tablespoon olive oil
• ½ cup green olives, pitted and halved
Preparation:
1. Put the olive oil into an Instant Pot and select the "Sauté" function.
2. Add the onions and mushrooms and cook for about 5 minutes.
3. Add in the tomato paste and garlic and cook for about 1 minute.
4. Stir in the olives, chicken, tomatoes, and broth and secure the lid.
5. Cook on high pressure for about 10 minutes.
6. Quickly release the pressure and stir in the parsley and black pepper.
7. Dish out and serve hot.
Serving Suggestions: Serve garnished with fresh dill.
Variation Tip: You can use black olives instead of green olives.
Nutritional Information per Serving:
Calories: 238|Fat: 9.7g|Sat Fat: 2.3g|Carbohydrates: 6.5g|Fiber: 1.5g|Sugar: 2.7g|Protein: 30.2g

Turkey and Sweet Potato Soup

Prep
Time: 10 Minutes
Cook Time: 30 Minutes
Serves: 4
Ingredients:
• 1 tablespoon olive oil
• 1 onion, chopped
• 2 celery stalks, chopped
• 2 teaspoons garlic, minced
• 4 cups cabbage, julienned
• 1 white sweet potato, skin removed and diced
• 8 cups chicken stock
• 2 bay leaves
• 1 cup turkey breast, cooked and chopped
• 2 teaspoons fresh thyme, chopped
• Himalayan pink salt, to taste

• Black pepper, to taste
Preparation:
1. Put the olive oil in a large pot over medium heat.
2. Add the onion, celery stalks, and garlic. Fry for 3 minutes until softened.
3. Add the cabbage and sweet potato and fry for 3 minutes.
4. Pour in the chicken stock, add the bay leaves, and bring to a boil.
5. Reduce the heat to low and simmer for 20 minutes until the vegetables are tender.
6. Add the cooked turkey and chopped thyme and simmer for 4 minutes until the turkey is heated through.
7. Remove the bay leaves and season the soup with ground Himalayan pink salt and black pepper.
Serving Suggestion: Top with chopped green onions.
Variation Tip: You can use chicken breasts instead of turkey breasts.
Nutritional Information per Serving:
Calories 325 | Fat 11g | Sodium 142mg | Carbs 30g | Fiber 4.2g | Sugar 8.6g | Protein 24g

Quinoa and Beef Soup

Prep Time: 10 Minutes
Cook Time: 30 Minutes
Serves: 4
Ingredients:
• 2 teaspoons olive oil
• 1 small red onion, chopped
• 1 tablespoon garlic, crushed
• 4 celery stalks with greens, chopped
• 2 medium carrots, peeled and diced
• 1 white sweet potato, peeled and diced
• 8 cups low-sodium beef broth
• 1 cup quinoa, cooked
• 2 cups beef cubes, cooked and cut
• 2 bay leaves
• 2 teaspoons sriracha sauce
• 2 teaspoons fresh thyme, chopped
• 1 cup kale, julienned
• Himalayan pink salt, to taste
• Black pepper, to taste
Preparation:
1. Place a large deep pot over medium-high heat and add the olive oil.
2. Fry the onion and garlic for 3 minutes until softened.
3. Add the celery, carrot, and sweet potato, and cook for 5 minutes, stirring occasionally.
4. Gently add the beef broth, cooked quinoa, beef cubes, bay leaves, and sriracha sauce.

5. Once the soup is boiling, reduce the heat to low. Simmer gently for 15 minutes until the vegetables are tender.
6. Discard the bay leaves and mix in the thyme and kale.
7. Continue to cook for 5 minutes and season with ground Himalayan pink salt and ground black pepper.
Serving Suggestion: Garnish with basil leaves.
Variation Tip: You can use farro, oats, or brown rice in place of the quinoa.
Nutritional Information per Serving:
Calories 345 | Fat 11g | Sodium 230mg | Carbs 33g | Fiber 5.9g | Sugar 4.5g | Protein 28g

Harvested Chicken Stew

Prep Time: 15 minutes
Cook Time: 30 minutes
Servings: 10
Ingredients:
• 2 cups boneless chicken breast meat, cooked and cubed
• 2 cups onions, chopped
• 1 cup celery, chopped
• 1½ cups carrot, sliced
• ½ cup corn
• 1 cup zucchini, sliced
• 2 cups whole peeled tomato
• 5 cups chicken broth
• ½ cup peas
Preparation:
1. Mix the chicken, celery, onions, tomatoes, corn, peas, zucchini, carrots, and broth in a large soup pot.
2. Thoroughly stir, then simmer for 30 minutes on medium-low heat.
3. Dish out and serve hot.
Serving Suggestions: You can serve the stew over cooked brown rice.
Variation Tip: You can add also add olives to this stew.
Nutritional Information per Serving:
Calories: 80|Fat: 1.3g|Sat Fat: 0.3g|Carbohydrates: 8.8g|Fiber: 2.2g|Sugar: 4.1g|Protein: 8.2g

Lamb Stew

Prep Time: 10 minutes
Cook Time: 40 minutes
Servings: 8
Ingredients:
• 1 small yellow onion, chopped
• 1 tablespoon olive oil
• 1 celery stalk, chopped
• 2 pounds grass-fed lamb shoulder, fat trimmed and cubed into 2-inch pieces
• 2 tablespoons sugar-free tomato paste
• 1 teaspoon dried oregano, crushed
• Salt and black pepper, to taste
• 1 red bell pepper, seeded and carved into 8 slices
• 1 tablespoon garlic, minced
• 2 cups fresh tomatoes, finely chopped
• 3 tablespoons fresh lemon juice
• 1 teaspoon dried basil, crushed
• ½ cup homemade chicken broth
• ¼ cup fresh parsley, minced
Preparation:
1. Sauté the olive oil and garlic in an Instant Pot for about 30 seconds, then add the onions.
2. Sauté for about 3 minutes, then stir in the rest of the ingredients except the parsley and bell peppers.
3. Secure the lid and cook on high pressure for about 20 minutes.
4. Naturally release the pressure for about 10 minutes, then quickly release the rest of the pressure.
5. Open the lid and add the bell peppers.
6. Cook for about 5 minutes and garnish with parsley to serve.
Serving Suggestions: Serve over boiled pasta.
Variation Tip: You can also use pork for this recipe.
Nutritional Information per Serving:
Calories: 279|Fat: 15.2g|Sat Fat: 5.2g|Carbohydrates: 5.4g|Fiber: 1.4g|Sugar: 3g|Protein: 29.2g

Omega-3-Rich Salmon Soup

Prep Time: 15 minutes
Cook Time: 30 minutes
Servings: 4
Ingredients:
• ½ cup celery stalk, chopped
• 1 tablespoon coconut oil
• 2 cups chicken broth
• 1 cup carrot, peeled and chopped
• 1 cup cauliflowers, chopped
• Salt and black pepper, to taste
• 1-pound salmon fillets
• ½ cup yellow onions, chopped
• ¼ cup fresh parsley, chopped
Preparation:
1. Heat the coconut oil in a wok and cook the salmon fillets for about 2 minutes on each side.
2. Add the carrots, onions, and cauliflower and cook for another 2 minutes.
3. Add the chicken broth, celery stalk, salt, and black pepper and secure the lid.
4. Cook on medium-low heat for 20 minutes, then remove the salmon fillets.
5. Cut the salmon into bite-sized chunks and put them back in the wok.
6. Simmer for 5 minutes and serve garnished with parsley.
Serving Suggestions: Serve topped with avocado slices.
Variation Tip: To add taste variation, you could add dried basil leaves.
Nutritional Information per Serving:
Calories: 225|Fat: 11.2g|Sat Fat: 4.1g|Carbohydrates: 6.5g|Fiber: 1.9g|Sugar: 3.1g|Protein: 25.5g

Poached Pears

Prep Time: 10 Minutes
Cook Time: 35 Minutes
Serves: 6
Ingredients:
• 6 pears, peeled
• 3 cups orange juice
• 1 teaspoon cardamom
• 1 cinnamon stick
• 1 star anise
Preparation:
1. Mix the orange juice, cardamom, cinnamon stick, and star anise in a saucepan.
2. Bring the liquid to a boil.
3. Add the peeled pears and close the lid.
4. Cook for 25 minutes on medium heat.
Serving Suggestion: Serve with ice cream.
Variation Tip: Substitute pears with apples.
Nutritional Information per Serving:
Calories 178 | Fat 0.6g | Sodium 4mg | Carbs 45g | Fiber 6.8g | Sugar 30.8g | Protein 1.6g

Berries and Cream

Prep Time: 15 minutes
Cook Time: 0 minutes
Servings: 6
Ingredients:
• 1 cup fresh blueberries

• 1½ cups fresh strawberries, sliced
• ¾ cup part-skim ricotta cheese
• ½ teaspoon Splenda
• 1½ tablespoons Marsala wine
• 1 tablespoon non-fat evaporated milk
• ½ cup cream
• 1½ tablespoons hazelnuts, toasted and chopped
Preparation:
1. Layer the blueberries and strawberries in 6 serving dishes.
2. Mix the ricotta cheese, cream, milk, wine, and sugar in a bowl.
3. Blend thoroughly with an electric beater.
4. Scoop a portion of the mixture over the fruit servings.
5. Top with toasted hazelnuts and serve chilled.
Serving Suggestions: Serve topped with berries and mint leaves.
Variation Tip: You can also use pecans instead of hazelnuts.
Nutritional Information per Serving:
Calories: 95|Fat: 4.5g|Sat Fat: 2.3g|Carbohydrates: 9.4g|Fiber: 1.4g|Sugar: 5.4g|Protein: 4.5g

Banana and Raspberry Mousse

Prep Time: 10 minutes
Cook Time: 0 minutes
Servings: 4
Ingredients:
• 2½ ounces raspberries, frozen
• 4 ounces banana, frozen
• Fresh berries, for topping
• 2 tablespoons stevia
• 4 egg whites
Preparation:
1. Put the egg whites and stevia in a blender and blend well.
2. Add the banana and berries and blend again.
3. Dish out into serving bowls and serve.
Serving Suggestions: Serve topped with a few fresh berries.
Variation Tip: You can also use strawberries in this recipe.
Nutritional Information per Serving:
Calories: 718|Fat: 0.6g|Sat Fat: 0.2g|Carbohydrates: 111.4g|Fiber: 1.3g|Sugar: 6.1g|Protein: 4.5g

Chocolate Yogurt Granita

Prep Time: 10 Minutes, plus freezing time
Cook Time: 0 Minutes
Serves: 4

Ingredients:
- 2 cups plain Greek yogurt
- ½ cup unsweetened almond milk
- ¼ cup unsweetened cocoa powder
- 2 tablespoons maple syrup
- 2 teaspoons pure vanilla extract

Preparation:
1. Place the yogurt, almond milk, cocoa powder, maple syrup, and vanilla in a blender and blend until very smooth.
2. Pour the mixture into a metal 9-inch square baking dish and place in the freezer.
3. Stir with a fork every 30 minutes or so for about 3 hours, until frozen and the mixture resembles soft snow.
4. Serve.

Serving Suggestion: Top with mint leaves.
Variation Tip: Add a tablespoon of peanut butter to the mixture for a varied taste.
Nutritional Information per Serving:
Calories 134 | Fat 3g | Sodium 93mg | Carbs 19g | Fiber 3g | Sugar 7.3g | Protein 8g

Apple Pie Parfait

Prep Time: 25 Minutes
Cook Time: 0 Minutes
Serves: 2

Ingredients:
- 1 apple, peeled, cored, and chopped
- 1 teaspoon maple syrup (optional)
- ½ teaspoon ground cinnamon
- 1 cup vanilla yogurt, divided
- ¼ cup chopped almonds or pecans, divided
- ¼ cup whipped coconut cream

Preparation:
1. In a small bowl, toss together the apple, maple syrup (if using), and cinnamon until well mixed.
2. Layer ¼ cup of yogurt in the bottom of a tall, wide glass or small bowl.
3. Then layer in ¼ of the apple and 1 tablespoon of almonds.
4. Repeat the layering and top the glass with 2 tablespoons of whipped coconut cream.
5. Repeat with a second glass or bowl and serve immediately.

Serving Suggestion: Garnish with mint.
Variation Tip: To make whipped coconut cream, take a chilled can of coconut milk and scoop off the top solid section into a medium bowl. Whip with electric hand beaters or a whisk until fluffy. You can add a dash of maple syrup if you want the cream a little sweeter, but it's equally delicious without.
Nutritional Information per Serving:
Calories 311 | Fat 20g | Sodium 87mg | Carbs 23g | Fiber 4g | Sugar 15g | Protein 9g

Lime and Coconut Truffles

Prep Time: 10 Minutes
Cook Time: 25 Minutes
Serves: 16 truffles

Ingredients:
- 8 ounces cream cheese, softened
- 1 lime, juiced and zested
- 7 drops liquid stevia
- ¼ cup coconut, shredded and toasted
- ¼ cup macadamia nuts
- ¼ teaspoons fine sea salt

Preparation:
1. In a medium mixing bowl, combine the softened cream cheese, lime juice, zest, and liquid stevia and mix well.
2. Cover with plastic wrap and place the bowl into the freezer for 10 minutes to chill.
3. Add the shredded coconut, macadamia nuts, fine sea salt to a food processor and pulse until finely ground. Transfer the mixture into a shallow dish.
4. Spoon the cream cheese mixture out of the bowl using a 1 tablespoon measuring spoon and roll into the coconut mixture to coat. Put the truffle in an airtight container.
5. Repeat to make 16 truffles. Place the container into the refrigerator for 15 minutes before serving.
6. Keep the truffles stored in the refrigerator.

Serving Suggestion: Serve with a chocolate sauce.
Variation Tip: You can roll these truffles in toasted crushed almonds and coconut.
Nutritional Information per Serving:
Calories 139 | Fat 14g | Sodium 143mg | Carbs 2g | Fiber 0.8g | Sugar 0.6g | Protein 3g

Berries with Vanilla Custard

Prep Time: 10 Minutes
Cook Time: 15 Minutes
Serves: 4
Ingredients:
- 1 cup half-and-half cream
- 2 large egg yolks
- 2 tablespoons sugar
- 2 teaspoons vanilla extract
- 2 cups fresh berries

Preparation:
1. Combine the cream, egg yolks, and sugar in a small heavy pot.
2. Cook while constantly stirring over low heat until the mixture is thick enough and a thermometer registers at least 160°F.
3. Transfer to a mixing bowl and add the vanilla extract.
4. Cover and refrigerate until cool.
Serving Suggestion: Serve with fresh berries on the side.
Variation Tip: Feel free to use any berry of your choice.
Nutritional Information per Serving:
Calories 166 | Fat 9g | Sodium 29mg | Carbs 16g | Fiber 2.5g | Sugar 11.4g | Protein 4g

Chili Grilled Pineapple

Prep Time: 10 Minutes
Cook Time: 10 Minutes
Serves: 6
Ingredients:
- 1 fresh pineapple, peeled and cored
- 3 tablespoons brown sugar
- 1 tablespoon lime juice
- 1 tablespoon olive oil
- 1 tablespoon honey
- 1 teaspoon chili powder
- Salt, to taste
Preparation:

1. Cut the pineapple lengthwise into 6 wedges.
2. Mix the remaining ingredients in a small bowl until well combined.
3. Brush half of the glaze on the pineapple, and save the rest for basting.
4. Broil the pineapple for 2–4 minutes on each side or until lightly browned (4 inches from the heat source).
5. Baste periodically with the leftover glaze.
Serving Suggestion: Garnish with mint leaves.
Variation Tip: Substitute honey with agave nectar.
Nutritional Information per Serving:
Calories 97 | Fat 2g | Sodium 34mg | Carbs 20g | Fiber 1g | Sugar 12.8g | Protein 1g

Chocolate Bombs

Prep Time: 40 minutes
Cook Time: 0 minutes
Servings: 4
Ingredients:
- 2 teaspoons vanilla extract
- 4 tablespoons heavy cream
- 4 tablespoons stevia
- ¼ cup natural chunky peanut butter
- 1 cup unrefined coconut oil
- ½ cup unsweetened cocoa powder
- 1¼ cups shelled hemp seeds
Preparation:
1. Mix cocoa powder, peanut butter, coconut oil, and hemp seeds in a large bowl. Combine well.
2. Add the cream, vanilla, and stevia and mix to form a paste.
3. Roll the mixture into balls and then dredge in the shredded coconut.
4. Organize the chocolate balls on a baking tray lined with parchment paper.
5. Put the baking tray in the freezer for about 10 minutes.
6. Transfer to the refrigerator for 30 minutes before serving.
Serving Suggestions: Serve with vanilla ice cream.
Variation Tip: You can use Splenda instead of stevia.
Nutritional Information per Serving:
Calories: 622|Fat: 68.2g|Sat Fat: 53.2g|Carbohydrates: 3.9g|Fiber: 1g|Sugar: 1.8g|Protein: 4.3g

Chocolate Greek Yogurt Ice Cream

Prep Time: 3 hours
Cook Time: 0 minutes
Servings: 4
Ingredients:
• 2 teaspoons vanilla extract
• 1 cup unsweetened almond milk
• 4 tablespoons stevia
• 1-ounce vanilla protein powder
• 5 ounces fat-free Greek yogurt
• 2 teaspoons unsweetened cocoa powder
Preparation:
1. Put the yogurt, protein powder, cocoa powder, stevia, and almond milk in a blender. Blend well.
2. Transfer the mixture to the freezer and freeze for 3 hours before serving.
Serving Suggestions: Serve with waffles.
Variation Tip: You can use coconut milk instead of almond milk.
Nutritional Information per Serving:
Calories: 100|Fat: 2.6g|Sat Fat: 0.9g|Carbohydrates: 11.1g|Fiber: 1.8g|Sugar: 7.8g|Protein: 7.9g

Pistachio Pie

Prep Time: 10 Minutes
Cook Time: 15 Minutes
Serves: 6
Ingredients:
• 4 ounces pistachio paste
• ½ cup almond flour
• 1 teaspoon vanilla extract
• ¼ teaspoon baking powder
• 2 tablespoons whole-grain flour
• 1 tablespoon liquid honey
Preparation:
1. Preheat the oven to 365℉.
2. Blend the almond flour, vanilla extract, baking powder, honey, and whole-grain flour in a food processor. Knead the mixture into a soft, non-sticky dough.
3. Put the dough in a round baking pan and flatten it into the shape of pie crust using your fingertips.
4. Spread the pie crust with the pistachio paste.
5. Bake the pie in the preheated oven for 15 minutes or until the edges are light brown.
Serving Suggestion: Top with crushed pistachios.
Variation Tip: Substitute honey with maple syrup.
Nutritional Information per Serving:
Calories 172 | Fat 12.9g | Sodium 35mg | Carbs 12.7g | Fiber 1.8g | Sugar 7.9g | Protein 3.3g

Lemonade Strawberry Popsicles

Prep Time: 3 hours
Cook Time: 0 minutes
Servings: 4
Ingredients:
• 8 ounces fresh lemon juice
• 3 pounds strawberries
• 10 drops liquid stevia
• 8 ounces low-fat cottage cheese
• ½ cup old-fashioned oats
Preparation:
1. Put the oats in a blender and blend well to form a powder.
2. Add the strawberries, lemon juice, cottage cheese, stevia, and blend well.
3. Carefully pour the mixture into popsicle molds and put them in the freezer.
4. Freeze for about 3 hours before serving.
Serving Suggestions: Serve with extra strawberries on the side.
Variation Tip: You can use your preferred artificial sweetener.
Nutritional Information per Serving:
Calories: 106|Fat: 1.6g|Sat Fat: 0.6g|Carbohydrates: 18.1g|Fiber: 4g|Sugar: 9.1g|Protein: 5.9g

Crème Brûlée

Prep Time: 4 hours 30 minutes
Cook Time: 12 minutes
Servings: 4
Ingredients:
• 5 egg yolks
• 2 cups heavy cream
• 1 teaspoon Splenda
• 1 tablespoon vanilla extract
Preparation:
1. Preheat the oven to 395°F and grease 4 (6-ounce) ramekins.
2. Mix all the ingredients in a bowl and beat well.
3. Divide the mixture evenly between the ramekins and place them in the preheated oven.
4. Bake for about 12 minutes, then remove from the oven.
5. Let the ramekins cool, then cover each with plastic wrap.
6. Refrigerate for about 4 hours and serve chilled.
Serving Suggestions: You can serve with some whipped cream.
Variation Tip: You can use stevia instead of Splenda.
Nutritional Information per Serving:
Calories: 289|Fat: 27.8g|Sat Fat: 15.9g|Carbohydrates: 3.8g|Fiber: 0g|Sugar: 1.6g|Protein: 4.6g

Pumpkin Custard

Prep Time: 3 hours
Cook Time: 30 minutes

Servings: 6
Ingredients:
• 4 organic eggs, beaten
• 15 ounces canned pumpkin puree
• ½ cup heavy cream
• 1 teaspoon stevia liquid cinnamon
• ¼ teaspoon salt
• 2 teaspoons vanilla extract
• 2 teaspoons pumpkin pie spice
Preparation:
1. Mix all the ingredients in a bowl and beat well.
2. Pour the mixture into a pan and cook for 30 minutes on medium-low heat, occasionally stirring.
3. Dish out into serving bowls and refrigerate for about 3 hours before serving.
Serving Suggestions: Serve topped with whipped cream.
Variation Tip: You can make this recipe with apricots too.
Nutritional Information per Serving:
Calories: 107|Fat: 6.9g|Sat Fat: 3.4g|Carbohydrates: 6.8g|Fiber: 2.1g|Sugar: 2.8g|Protein: 4.7g

Limeaba lemon Glaciate

Prep Time: 5 minutes
Cook Time: 0 minutes
Servings: 2
Ingredients:
• ½ ripe banana
• 1½ cups ice, crushed
• ½ lime, juiced
• 2 strawberries, as garnish
• ½ lemon, juiced
Preparation:
1. Blend the banana and ice together in a blender until smooth.
2. Add the lime juice and lemon juice and pour into serving glasses.
Serving Suggestions: Serve garnished with strawberries.
Variation Tip: You can also use cherries for garnishing.
Nutritional Information per Serving:
Calories: 48|Fat: 0.2g|Sat Fat: 0g|Carbohydrates: 13.1g|Fiber: 1.8g|Sugar: 4.2g|Protein: 0.6g

Almond Cake

Prep Time: 10 Minutes
Cook Time: 45 Minutes
Serves: 6

Ingredients:
- ⅔ cup almond flour
- ⅓ cup unsweetened applesauce
- 3 large eggs, yolks and whites separated
- 7 tablespoons stevia, divided
- 3 tablespoons unsalted organic butter, melted, divided
- 1 teaspoon vanilla extract or essence
- ¼ teaspoon almond extract
- ⅛ teaspoon fine sea salt
- ½ cup almonds, sliced and toasted

Preparation:
1. Preheat the oven to 350°F
2. Brush a 7-inch cake pan with 1 tablespoon of melted butter and sprinkle 1 tablespoon of stevia to form a thin coating on the bottom. Set aside.
3. In a stand mixer fitted with a paddle attachment, mix the almond flour, applesauce, egg yolks, 3 tablespoons of stevia, 2 tablespoons of melted butter, vanilla, almond extract, and salt until well combined.
4. Using a hand mixer, beat the egg whites in a medium bowl for 3–5 minutes until soft peaks form.
5. Add and whisk in 3 tablespoons of stevia.
6. Using a silicone spatula, gently fold the egg whites into the yolk mixture until well combined. Pour the batter into the prepared cake pan.
7. Bake for 45 minutes in the preheated oven, or until the top is lightly browned and a toothpick inserted into the middle comes out clean.
8. Let the cake cool on a cooling rack.
9. In the meantime, scatter the sliced almonds onto a microwave-safe plate and microwave for 1½ minutes to toast.
10. Sprinkle the toasted almonds on the cooled cake.

Serving Suggestion: You can dust the cake with powdered sugar and add some fresh berries or make a berry compote.

Variation Tip: Substitute almonds with pistachios or cashews.

Nutritional Information per Serving:
Calories 184 | Fat 16g | Sodium 169mg | Carbs 9g | Fiber 14g | Sugar 2.1g | Protein 7g

4-Week Diet Plan

Week 1

Day 1:
Breakfast: Pomegranate Porridge
Lunch: Harvested Chicken Stew
Snack: Paprika Roasted Pecans
Dinner: Turkey Meatballs
Dessert: Pistachio Pie

Day 2:
Breakfast: Strawberry and Ricotta Pancakes
Lunch: White Mushroom Soup
Snack: Asian Green Triangles
Dinner: Healthy Oven-Fried Pork Chops
Dessert: Berries and Cream

Day 3:
Breakfast: Cottage Cheese Pancakes
Lunch: Fish Stew
Snack: Chicken Nuggets
Dinner: Cheesy Chicken Casserole
Dessert: Lemonade Strawberry Popsicles

Day 4:
Breakfast: Egg Muffins
Lunch: Baked Sea Bass
Snack: Mexican Jicama Snack
Dinner: Lemon Chicken Piccata
Dessert: Chili Grilled Pineapple

Day 5:
Breakfast: Blueberry Overnight Oats
Lunch: Glazed Scallops
Snack: Jicama Snack
Dinner: Tarragon Soup
Dessert: Chocolate Yogurt Granita

Day 6:
Breakfast: Asparagus Omelet
Lunch: Herbed Halibut
Snack: Spinach Chips
Dinner: Harvested Chicken Stew
Dessert: Apple Pie Parfait

Day 7:
Breakfast: Smoked Salmon and Cream Cheese Wraps
Lunch: Pan-Roasted Broccoli
Snack: Baked Banana Chips
Dinner: Strawberry-Lemon Thyme Soup
Dessert: Berries With Vanilla Custard

Week 2

Day 1:
Breakfast: Bulgur Porridge
Lunch: Chicken Arroz
Snack: Grilled Veggie Wrap
Dinner: Curry Pork Chops
Dessert: Banana and Raspberry Mousse

Day 2:
Breakfast: Chickpea Flour Omelet
Lunch: Chili-Lime Mushroom Tacos
Snack: Air Fryer Plantain Chips
Dinner: Curry Pork Chops
Dessert: Almond Cake

Day 3:
Breakfast: Egg Muffins with Turkey and Bacon
Lunch: Vegetarian Black Bean Pasta
Snack: Baked Carrot
Dinner: Chicken and Green Bean Curry
Dessert: Pistachio Pie

Day 4:
Breakfast: Cottage Cheese Pancakes
Lunch: Cheesy Cauli Bake
Snack: Jicama Snack
Dinner: Chicken Cacciatore
Dessert: Chocolate Yogurt Granita

Day 5:
Breakfast: Whipped Cottage Cheese Breakfast Bowl
Lunch: Cheesy Cauli Bake
Snack: Paprika Roasted Pecans
Dinner: White Mushroom Soup
Dessert: Chili Grilled Pineapple

Day 6:
Breakfast: Quinoa Breakfast Bowl
Lunch: Tofu Stir-Fry
Snack: Asian Green Triangles
Dinner: Kale and Cauliflower Soup
Dessert: Lime and Coconut Truffles

Day 7:
Breakfast: Bulgur Porridge
Lunch: Cauliflower Fried Rice
Snack: Grilled Veggie Wrap
Dinner: Broccoli and Asparagus Soup
Dessert: Almond Cake

Week 3

Day 1:
Breakfast: Blueberry Overnight Oats
Lunch: Mushroom Stroganoff
Snack: Parsnip Fries
Dinner: Chicken Dill Soup
Dessert: Apple Pie Parfait

Day 2:
Breakfast: Pomegranate Porridge
Lunch: Lemony Brussels Sprouts
Snack: Spinach Chips
Dinner: Kale and Cauliflower Soup
Dessert: Banana and Raspberry Mousse

Day 3:
Breakfast: Buckwheat Crepes
Lunch: Cheesy Cauli Bake
Snack: Paprika Chickpeas
Dinner: Harvested Chicken Stew
Dessert: Chocolate Yogurt Granita

Day 4:
Breakfast: Peach Pancakes
Lunch: Lemon and Garlic Green Beans
Snack: Asian Green Triangles
Dinner: Chicken Chili
Dessert: Banana and Raspberry Mousse

Day 5:
Breakfast: Egg Muffins with Turkey and Bacon
Lunch: Cheesy Cauli Bake
Snack: Air Fryer Plantain Chips
Dinner: Chicken Cordon Bleu
Dessert: Chocolate Greek Yogurt Ice Cream

Day 6:
Breakfast: Cottage Cheese Pancakes
Lunch: Roasted Vegetable Strata
Snack: Mexican Jicama Snack
Dinner: Turkey Tacos
Dessert: Chili Grilled Pineapple

Day 7:
Breakfast: Cauliflower Oatmeal
Lunch: Vegetarian Black Bean Pasta
Snack: Spinach Chips
Dinner: Spicy Lamb Casserole
Dessert: Chocolate Bombs

Week 4

Day 1:
Breakfast: Buckwheat Crepes
Lunch: Endive and Sweet Potato Bake
Snack: Paprika Chickpeas
Dinner: Chicken Dill Soup
Dessert: Lime and Coconut Truffles

Day 2:
Breakfast: Chickpea Flour Omelet
Lunch: Roasted Beans and Green Onions
Snack: Asian Green Triangles
Dinner: White Mushroom Soup
Dessert: Chili Grilled Pineapple

Day 3:
Breakfast: Asparagus Omelet
Lunch: Spaghetti Squash
Snack: Chicken Nuggets
Dinner: Lemon Chicken Piccata
Dessert: Poached Pears

Day 4:
Breakfast: Blueberry Overnight Oats
Lunch: Pan-Roasted Broccoli
Snack: Grilled Veggie Wrap
Dinner: Zesty Salmon
Dessert: Chili Grilled Pineapple

Day 5:
Breakfast: Egg Muffins with Turkey and Bacon
Lunch: Mashed Butternut Squash
Snack: Air Fryer Plantain Chips
Dinner: Citrus Glazed Salmon
Dessert: Chili Grilled Pineapple

Day 6:
Breakfast: Cottage Cheese Pancakes
Lunch: Veggie Chili
Snack: Parsnip Fries
Dinner: Sweet and Sour Fish
Dessert: Berries and Cream

Day 7:
Breakfast: Cauliflower Oatmeal
Lunch: Cumin Quinoa Patties
Snack: Baked Carrot
Dinner: Chicken Cacciatore
Dessert: Pumpkin Custard

Conclusion

Type -2 diabetes is a chronic condition in which the body controls and uses glucose for fat. These long-term infections cause too much sugar in the arteries. Finally, high blood sugar can damage blood vessels, the nervous system, and the immune system. There is no cure for type 2 diabetes mellitus, but weight loss, eating a healthy diet, and exercising can help control the disease.

The best way to control your diabetes is healthy living with proper exercise and walking for 30 minutes to 1 hour a day. Drink water regularly and keep yourself hydrated. Eat healthy low carbs and steep out fat and sodium from your daily food intake. For your health always choose high-quality proteins, a vitamin-rich diet, and dietary fiber in your diet. This leads you to manage your healthy lifestyle, weight loss as well as manage type-2 diabetes.

This amazing cookbook will help you to regulate your healthy eating habits as it can be restricted to what to eat and what not. The amazing diet plans in the book help you manage to eat healthy as well as the yummy food for managing a healthy lifestyle and remission your type-2 diabetes.

This unique cookbook is specially designed under the supervision of nutritionists and doctors and it completely guides you to have a healthy full meal all day long from yummy breakfast to delicious snacks as well. The diet plan and the motivation encourage you to set your healthy lifestyle without worrying about this situation. Go grab the wonderful "Type-2 Diabetes cookbook" now and start living healthy.

Appendix Measurement Conversion Chart

WEIGHT EQUIVALENTS

US STANDARD	METRIC (APPROXINATE)
1 ounce	28 g
2 ounces	57 g
5 ounces	142 g
10 ounces	284 g
15 ounces	425 g
16 ounces (1 pound)	455 g
1.5pounds	680 g
2pounds	907 g

VOLUME EQUIVALENTS (DRY)

US STANDARD	METRIC (APPROXIMATE)
⅛ teaspoon	0.5 mL
¼ teaspoon	1 mL
½ teaspoon	2 mL
¾ teaspoon	4 mL
1 teaspoon	5 mL
1 tablespoon	15 mL
¼ cup	59 mL
½ cup	118 mL
¾ cup	177 mL
1 cup	235 mL
2 cups	475 mL
3 cups	700 mL
4 cups	1 L

TEMPERATURES EQUIVALENTS

FAHRENHEIT(F)	CELSIUS（C） (APPROXIMATE)
225 °F	107 °C
250 °F	120 °C
275 °F	135 °C
300 °F	150 °C
325 °F	160 °C
350 °F	180 °C
375 °F	190 °C
400 °F	205 °C
425 °F	220 °C
450 °F	235 °C
475 °F	245 °C
500 °F	260 °C

VOLUME EQUIVALENTS (LIQUID)

US STANDARD	US STANDARD (OUNCES)	METRIC (APPROXIMATE)
2 tablespoons	1 fl.oz	30 mL
¼ cup	2 fl.oz	60 mL
½ cup	4 fl.oz	120 mL
1 cup	8 fl.oz	240 mL
1½ cup	12 fl.oz	355 mL
2 cups or 1 pint	16 fl.oz	475 mL
4 cups or 1 quart	32 fl.oz	1 L
1 gallon	128 fl.oz	4 L

Made in the USA
Las Vegas, NV
13 April 2022

47347177R00044